PERIOD HOUSES AND THEIR DETAILS

Chimney-piece in the Cube-Room, Sudbrook Park, Petersham, Surrey

PERIOD HOUSES AND THEIR DETAILS

Edited by *COLIN AMERY*

BUTTERWORTH ARCHITECTURE

London   Singapore   Sydney   Wellington

First published 1974 in Great Britain by The Architectural Press,
This reprint published by Butterworth Architecture,
an imprint of Butterworth Scientific
PART OF REED INTERNATIONAL P.L.C.

First paperback edition 1978
Reprinted 1982, 1986, 1988

© Butterworth Architecture 1974

ISBN 0 85139 515 5 (paper)

Printed and bound in Great Britain by
Anchor Brendon Ltd., Tiptree, Essex

ACKNOWLEDGMENTS

IN the first place the debt must be acknowledged which is owed to the draughts-men who originally drew the working drawings in this book and whose names are appended at the foot of each drawing. The excellent quality of the work done by the craftsmen of bygone days is clearly revealed by these meticulous drawings. Acknowledgment is also due to Bill Toomey (The Architectural Press) for a series of photographs specially taken for this book, as follows: Plates 1, 23, 26, 33, 35, 38, 41, 49, 67, 69, 71, 73, 75, 78, 79, 89 (lower), 96, 98, 102, 162, 181, 184, 190, 192 and 193. Thanks are due, too, to Dan Cruickshank for his advice and help when this book was being compiled.

The following kindly gave permission for copyright photographs to be reproduced, as listed below:

The Victoria and Albert Museum, South Kensington (Crown Copyright): Plates 6, 29, 55, 114, 116, 117, 120, 122, 126, 128, 133, 134, 136, 138, 142 and 188. The Greater London Council (Department of Architecture and Civic Design): Plates 9, 10 and 158. The National Monuments Record, London: Plates 17 and 63. Ashby and Horner Ltd (Builders), London: Plate 31. *Country Life*, London: Plates 108, 146, 151 and 154. The Ashmolean Museum, University of Oxford: Plate 110. The Metropolitan Water Division of The Thames Water Authority, London: Plate 174. The Department of the Environment and The Public Record Office, London: Plate 176. The Chiswick Central Library, Hounslow: Plate 205.

Finally, thanks must be expressed to the following who have allowed details of their houses to be photographed or who have helped in various ways: Benson and Benson, architects, Chiswick; The Curator, Sir John Soane's Museum, London; the Grosvenor Estate, London; the Honourable Society of the Inner Temple, London; Mallett at Bourdon House Ltd., London; Mr J. Milnes-Smith, Department of Architecture and Civic Design, G.L.C.; the Montfort Missionaries, Cromwell House, Highgate; the Public Record Office, London; the Registrar General, Somerset House, London; the Richmond Golf Club, Sudbrook Park, Petersham, Surrey; the Welsh Office, Whitehall, London.

LIST OF PLATES

INTRODUCTION

WHEN *The Architectural Review* began to publish a series of measured drawings and photographs of fine old buildings, early in this century, it had a very specific purpose in mind. Under the somewhat stern title, *The Practical Exemplar of Architecture*, the series was intended to illustrate 'fine Examples and Details for the use of those who desire to study the work of the masters in Architectural Design and Construction'. The examples chosen were not merely to provide a permanent record of fine buildings and details but 'to place in the hands of the practising architect a number of graphic reproductions inspiring emulation, suggesting motifs and showing forms and methods adaptable to current uses'.

In reissuing a selection of these fine drawings, the aim here is perhaps more general. Today, the value of the measured drawing is not so much to inspire emulation but rather to provide the best way of learning how to understand a building. A detailed drawing studied at leisure, especially when accompanied by a photograph, is the closest one can get to understanding a building, short of visiting it to measure and draw the actual structure. Thus it is to be hoped that this book of drawings will serve as an armchair guide leading to a better understanding of the smaller historic buildings with which it deals. These are confined to domestic work of the late-seventeenth and eighteenth centuries only. For *The Practical Exemplar,** edited by the late Sir Mervyn Macartney, eventually filled seven bulky portfolios covering a vast field, ranging from details of the smallest garden temple to those of a massive nineteenth-century town hall, and it was therefore necessary to limit this book to one building type only and to exclude anything earlier than Jacobean or later than Regency. A further reason which governed this selection was the anticipation that this book will be the first of a series, as there is much additional material to be extracted from the deep mine of the original *Exemplar*. Ecclesiastical furnishings, market crosses, monuments and tombstones, as well as a fascinating series of classical colonnades, cornices and ceilings, are only some of the subjects with which future volumes could deal.

The buildings shown here are of a kind to be seen in every British city or small town—buildings you may not notice at first, unless your eye is caught by a fine doorway or an elegant piece of wrought ironwork. A few are not so modest: Sudbrook Park, Petersham, Surrey (*Plates 108–113*), designed by James Gibbs, reaches such a height of sumptuousness in its Cube Room that it

---

* *The Practical Exemplar of Architecture,* edited by the late Sir Mervyn Macartney, FSA, FRIBA, first ran as a series (starting in 1906 and continuing into the 'twenties) in *The Architectural Review*. Later, it was published by The Architectural Press in seven loose-leaf portfolios, brought out periodically. The final portfolio (the seventh) was published in 1927

can hardly be called a minor domestic work. But most of the buildings fall into the category of small houses that are all distinguished by the high standard of craftsmanship to be seen in their details. These reprinted drawings have an extra value today when most new buildings are totally devoid of both decoration and craftsmanship. Apart from the visual pleasure afforded by this selection, it is to be hoped that they will also be of value to architects and others concerned with the restoration of old houses and historic buildings.

As with the eighteenth-century pattern books, these drawings consist of a collection of design experiences. Every detail has within it a certain amount of trial and error, a certain amount of design skill and a modicum of luck. By collecting together a series of measured drawings of historic buildings it is possible to see how architects learned from each other and from the past. It is also possible to compare the vitality of the craftsmanship. For example, some of the doorways built early in the eighteenth century show all the signs of the personal involvement of the craftsman, whereas some of the ones built later in that century are clearly copied from the pattern books and lack the style of the Queen Anne doorways. However, it should also be added that, to our modern eyes, ordinary 'run-of-the-mill Georgian' has acquired a lofty status and succeeds, as architecture, because it respects our humanity to an astonishing degree.

What shines forth from the pages that follow is the degree of consideration given by builders and architects to both the function and the appearance of their buildings. Isaac Ware gives an instance of this in *A Complete Body of Architecture*. Writing in 1756 and discussing the eighteenth-century architect's approach to his art, he said:

'Here is a space to be covered with building: and the great consideration is its division into parts, for different uses; and their distribution. In this regard is to be had two things, the convenience of the inhabitant and the beauty and proportion of the fabrick. Neither of these should be considered independently of the other, because if it be, the other will not fail to be sacrificed to it; and this, which would be very disagreeable, is never absolutely necessary'.

Eighteenth-century houses, particularly those we now call Georgian town houses, are the perfect embodiment of this attitude of mind. The words of an earlier writer than Ware, one John Neave, reflect the same attitude. In 1707, in his *Country Purchaser,* when praising the new style of architecture for its successful fusion of planning and design, he said that 'the genius of our time is altogether for light staircases, fine sash windows and lofty ceilings. And such has been of late our builders' industry, in point of compactness and uniformity, that a house after the new way will afford upon the same quantity of ground much more space and conveniences'.

Eighteenth-century domestic architecture, particularly between 1715 and 1730, was stable and uniform. The Palladian gospel had been spread by the pattern books. These books were compiled by carpenters like William Halfpenny of Twickenham or the carpenter/architect, Batty Langley, and they were full of good drawings of details and the orders and contained accurate plates of doors, windows and other elements. Sold to both the gentry and craftsmen, they spread the word of self-improvement. Batty Langley, in 1741, in the introduction to his book, *The City and country Workman's Treasury of Design, or the Art of Drawing and Working the Ornamental Parts of Architecture*, explained his motives thus:

'The great Pleasure that Builders and Workmen of all kinds have of late years taken in the Study of Architecture; and the great advantages that have accrued to those, for whom they have been employed; by having their works executed in a much neater and more magnificent manner than was ever done in this Kingdom before; has been the real motive that induced me, to the compiling of this Work, for their further Improvement'.

This book has a more subtle motive than Batty Langley's. It is to 'improve' the reader by encouraging him to look afresh at these buildings. For, by looking at them with an added knowledge of the skilful details, it is possible to come close to that compromise between seeing and knowing that can help both the practice and appreciation of good architecture.

The illustrations in this book are arranged in sections, beginning with a series of exteriors. These are followed by a collection of handsome doorways, and then by a smaller group of drawings and photographs of gateways and ironwork. The interiors are arranged together and the details of the interiors —chimney-pieces and staircases—follow as separate sections.

The first section—exteriors—includes examples of work by Inigo Jones (*Plates 1–5*), and a remarkable house, wrongly attributed to Wren, that has somehow managed to survive in Croydon (*Plates 23–25*). The fine cornice from an old house in the Strand (*Plates 9–10*) is being looked after by the Historic Buildings Division of the Greater London Council; but, rather sadly, it is stored out of sight. Moulinière House (*Plates 21–22*), an elegant home built for Huguenot refugees, was demolished soon after the 1914–18 War. The shopfront in Artillery Lane, Spitalfields (*Plates 31–32*), is altogether a happier story, however. It was completely repaired and restored in 1973 and stands in a derelict part of London as a clear demonstration of the value of careful conservation.

The examples in the section on doorways represent the amazing diversity that was achieved with a fixed tradition of English building. From the late seventeenth-century shell porch at Bocking, Essex (*Plates 59–62*), to the simple everyday eighteenth-century doorways in Reading (*Plates 81–84*), there can be seen a rigorous standard of excellent craftsmanship at work. These doorways are the eye-catchers of the plain fronted houses. Although some of them were fairly routine pieces of joinery when they were built, they now appear outstanding among their bland machine-made modern equivalents. Also, what can still be seen is the gauged brickwork of the pediments and pilasters of the houses in King's Bench Walk in the Temple, London (*Plates 33–40*). Simply by cutting the bricks the craftsman has brilliantly enlivened these simple doorways.

Stanley Ramsey, writing in his introduction to *Small Houses of the Late Georgian Period: 1750–1820*, Volume II, drew attention to the fact that, although not everyone is moved by the exteriors of the period, they do appreciate the interiors. 'Even those critics', he wrote, 'who do not love the work of the late Georgian period, and look askance at its "dull, uninteresting facades", will, in their less guarded moments, grudgingly admit that much of the interior decoration of the period has great charm and beauty'. The interiors selected for this book cover a wide period and range from the magnificence of Gibbs's Sudbrook Park, (*Plates 108–113*), to the small scale elegance of Bourdon House, Berkeley Square (*Plates 146–157*). Much space has been devoted to one house, No. 26 Hatton Garden (*Plates 114–145*), now sadly demolished, as the measured drawings and photographs do give a full record of the interior of an early eighteenth-century London house. The quality of the carving and panelling can still be appreciated in the one room that has been preserved in the Victoria and Albert Museum.

Chimney-pieces merit a special section because of the quality and range of the examples chosen by the original compilers of *The Practical Exemplar*. The ebullient example of a Jacobean carved chimney-piece once stood in a house in the City of London (*Plates 166–171*). Such vigorous carving makes this a very rare and treasured survival. Solid oak splendour is to be seen in the Grinling Gibbons chimney-piece now tucked away in the offices of the Metropolitan Water Board in Islington, London (*Plates 172–175*). Excellence of a far more chaste and subtle kind is displayed in Sir John Soane's little fireplace designed for his own house in London (*Plates 190–191*).

As for staircases, space only allows the inclusion of a few good examples. Hopefully, the plainer eighteenth-century ones will not be eclipsed by the lively representatives of the New Model Army that adorn the staircase at Cromwell House, Highgate, London (*Plates 192–198*).

Taken as a whole the drawings in this book—so well executed by the draughtsmen concerned—clearly show the richness of English domestic architecture and the skills of the unknown craftsmen of the past. Today, how few are those who will ever experience the joy of living in an old house, or be able to sense the care and craftsmanship that can give the simplest building a rare personal quality. One man who did know the value of an old house was the poet, Robert Southey, who wrote the following in a letter to his friend G. C. Bedford, in 1803:

'I am glad to hear that you have got a house, and still more, that it is an old house. I love old houses best, for the sake of the odd closets and cupboards and good thick walls that don't let the wind blow in, and little out-of-the-way poly-angular rooms with great beams running across the ceiling—the old heart of oak, that has outlasted half a score generations; and chimney-pieces with the date of the year carved above them, and huge fireplaces that warmed the shins of Englishmen before the House of Hanover came over. The most delightful associations that ever made me feel, and think, and fall a-dreaming, are excited by old buildings—not absolute ruins but in a state of decline. Even the clipt yews interest me: and if I found one in any garden that should become mine, in the shape of a peacock, I should be as proud to keep his tail well spread as the man who first carved him. In truth I am more disposed to connect myself by sympathy with the ages that are past, and by hope with those that are to come, than to vex and irritate myself by any lively interest about the existing generation. . . .'

It is to be hoped that the existing generation of architects and the growing numbers of those who appreciate old buildings will be helped by this book to look more closely at the buildings of their own towns and villages. Since enough buildings have been recklessly demolished and replaced by a sea of mediocrity in our towns, it is perhaps possible that this book will arouse a detailed interest in the quality of our surroundings, and an active concern for the conservation of our architectural heritage.*

London 1974   C.A.

---

* It is sad but necessary to record that the following houses included in this book have been demolished: *Exteriors:* House at Enfield, Essex (*Plate 6*); Houses in the Strand, London (*Plates 9–11*); Mouliniére House, Wandsworth, London (*Plate 21*); 15 Cornhill, London (shopfront preserved) (*Plate 29*). *Doorways:* 33 Mark Lane, London (Spanish Embassy) (*Plate 46*); House in Carey Street, Westminster (*Plate 55*); House at Bocking, Essex, (due for demolition) (*Plate 59*); St. Anselms, Croydon (by enemy action) (*Plate 65*); 16 and 17 Friar Street, Reading (*Plates 81–84*). *Interiors:* No. 26, Hatton Garden, London (*Plates 114–145*). *Chimney-pieces:* House in Coleman Street, London (*Plate 166*). *Staircases:* House in Botolph Lane, London (*Plate 199*); Brent House, Brentford, London (*Plate 205*); 28 Margaret Street, Westminster (*Plate 211*).

Exteriors

Notes on Plates 1–32

Plates 1–5

57 and 58 Lincoln's Inn Fields, London.

Usually known as 'Lindsey House', this is certainly an early Stuart house and is probably by Inigo Jones (1640). It is difficult to say how much of the original house remains. It was divided into two in 1751–2 and it has no surviving Jones' interiors. What remains agrees to some extent with the plate published by Colen Campbell in *Virtruvius Britannicus*. The great pilasters have no entasis and they rest firmly on a broad band of stone, which acts as a finish to the fine rusticated ground-floor storey. The top balustrade once supported urns.

Plates 6–8

Brickwork from a house at Enfield, Middlesex.

Once part of a late seventeenth-century house, the illustrations show a part of the façade that formed the centre of a recessed section of the first floor. All the superb detail was entirely carried out in gauged brickwork. The centre opening originally held a window, and the surrounding entablature, pilasters and other enrichments are all formed of cut and rubbed brickwork.

The house from which this façade came was the school where Keats was educated, and later on, when the railway first came to Enfield, it served as the station building. This brickwork is now in the Victoria and Albert Museum.

Plates 9–11

Cornices of Houses in the Strand, London.

These houses in the Strand no longer exist, alas, but the fine cornice of No 164a (the right-hand house in *Plate 9*) has been preserved by the Historic Buildings Division (Department of Architecture) of the Greater London Council. It is a sturdy example of late seventeenth-century work. Made of wood, it is heavily ornamented with consoles and is blocked and enriched with carving. It was remarkable, when insitu, as its scale was exactly right for the old Strand houses. Just this fragment gives some idea of the quality of the buildings that lined the once elegant link between Westminster and the City.

Plate 11 illustrates the cornice of another demolished house in a different part of the Strand.

Plates 12–16

The School House, Risley, Derbyshire.

Erected in 1706, this building is the work of an unknown architect. Whoever he was, he had a great enthusiasm for his materials, and the result is a façade full of vigour and variety. It is a rich mixture of rubbed and gauged brickwork and well-cut Derbyshire stone. The steeply pitched roof has warm tiles and lead trim on the hips. It is the doorway that dominates on the entrance façade, and the detail in the measured drawings shows the elaborate nature of the carvings.

Plates 17–20

The Judge's Lodging, St Giles, Oxford.

This ashlar-faced house was built in 1702. A plate on the roof is inscribed 'Thomas Rowney Esq, Elizabeth his wife, Anne 1702' (presumably a record of the first owner). The front is symmetrically designed with rusticated angles and a cornice, and the central bay has a pediment. The windows have architraves and the ground-floor ones have cornices also. The front doorway has been altered since first constructed. The forecourt of the house has stone gate piers and angle piers surmounted by cornices and vases, and the wrought-iron entrance gates have an ornamented band and cresting.

Plate 19 shows the doorway at the back, into the garden. It has a half-domed hood supported on brackets and decorated with a cherub's head, scrolls and a basket of fruit and flowers.

Plates 21–22

Moulinère House, Wandsworth, London.

Moulinère House was built around 1700 and was occupied by a French Huguenot family who gave the house their name. In 1738 it was valued at £22. It has had a series of interesting owners, including the Duchess of Marlborough and the architect Robert Billings (1813–74) who restored buildings and kept his large private museum in the house. Originally standing in open country near the village of Wandsworth, the house gradually became engulfed in the tangle of main roads around Putney. After a rather ignominious period as a laundry it was demolished soon after the first World War. Christopher Woodbridge's fine drawing reveals the simple elegance of the proportions of the main façade and the attractive brickwork.

Plates 23–25
Wrencote, Croydon, Surrey.
The house was built about 1720, or possibly slightly earlier. Although attributed to Sir Christopher Wren, there seems to be no proof whatever that he designed it. It is chiefly remarkable for the quality of its brickwork and the elaborate nature of the cornice which is shown in the detail drawing (*Plate 25*). The house is the best period house in Croydon, but it has now been almost submerged by the tall buildings of the newly developed town centre. It has also lost the railings which once embellished its forecourt (see *Plate 100*).

Plates 26–28
Oriel Window, Hogarth House, Chiswick, London.
A charming example of the art of eighteenth-century building, this attractive oriel window enlivens the plain garden front of the house that Hogarth called his 'little country box'. He must often have sat in the bay looking down onto his famous mulberry tree; but now he would be deafened by the roar of passing motorway traffic. The window is built out onto projecting joists and the entire oriel is made only of wood which is neatly fashioned and moulded in a simple craftsmanlike way that has totally vanished from today's buildings.

Plates 29–30
Shopfront formerly at 15 Cornhill, London.
This shopfront for an eighteenth-century coffee house was removed to the Victoria and Albert Museum, South Kensington, when No 15 Cornhill was demolished. The detail drawing was done when the shopfront was still standing in Cornhill. Although now transferred to Angel Court in the City, Birch's restaurant still functions, and it has wisely retained its eighteenth-century traditions by fronting its new home with a good reproduction of the original shopfront.

Plates 31–32
Shopfront at 56 Artillery Lane, London.
In 1973, the firm of architects, Benson and Benson, restored some early eighteenth-century houses in Artillery Lane. The building firm of Ashby and Horner carried out the work. An important operation was the repairing of the shopfront of No 56, the date of which is probably about 1756. A comparison of *Plate 31* (a recent photograph) with *Plate 32* (drawn before the restoration) shows that the work has been skilfully done. The first-floor ironwork and the railings in front of the door on the right were too decayed to repair, but otherwise this shopfront has been returned to the same condition as when it was first built by a prosperous wool merchant, and it provides a salutary example of the way these old shopfronts should be repaired rather than destroyed.
Situated in a rather run-down area east of the City, this is one of the finest eighteenth-century shopfronts in London.

Plate 1

Exteriors.

Nos. 57 and 58, Lincoln's Inn Fields, London.

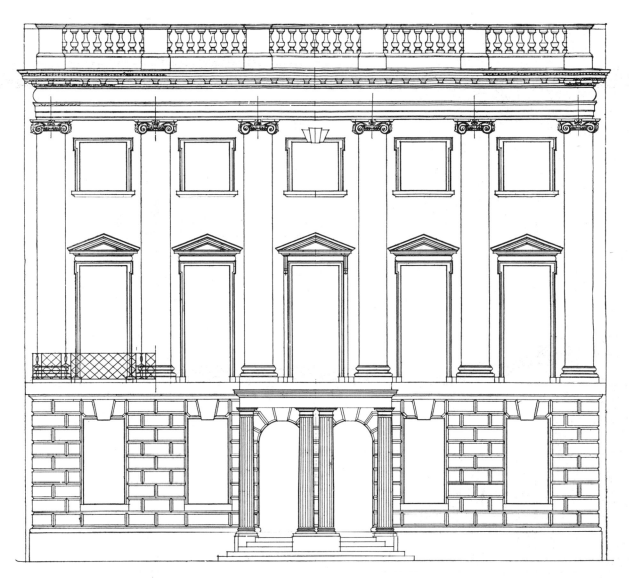

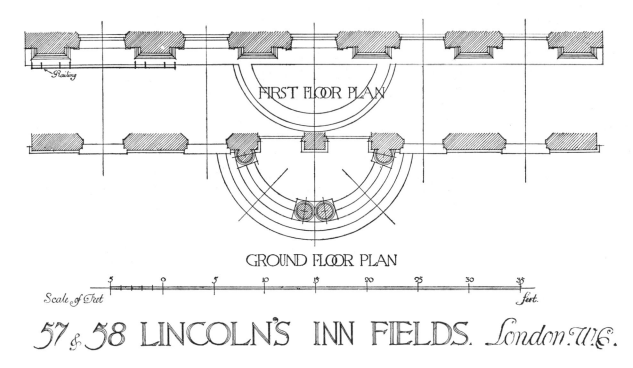

FIRST FLOOR PLAN

GROUND FLOOR PLAN

Scale of Feet   feet.

57 & 58 LINCOLN'S INN FIELDS. London. W.C.

Measured by H. A. McQueen and Ernst V. West.   Drawn by H. A. McQueen.

Plate 3   Exteriors.

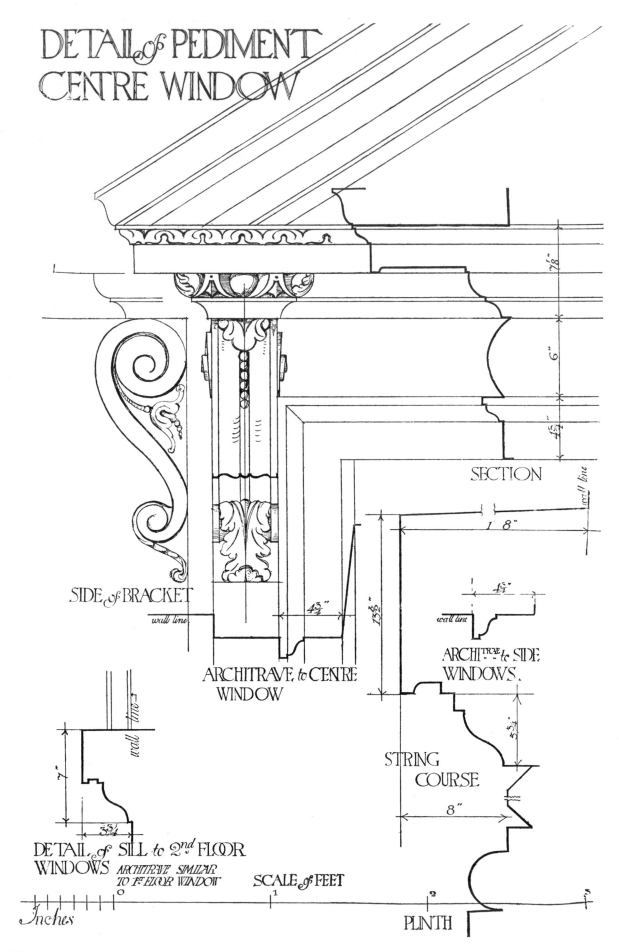

DETAIL of PEDIMENT
CENTRE WINDOW

SECTION

SIDE of BRACKET

wall line

ARCHITRAVE to CENTRE
WINDOW

ARCHITRAVE to SIDE
WINDOWS.

STRING
COURSE

DETAIL of SILL to 2nd FLOOR
WINDOWS ARCHITRAVE SIMILAR
TO 1st FLOOR WINDOW

SCALE of FEET

Inches

PLINTH

Nos. 57 and 58, Lincoln's Inn Fields, London.

Measured by H. A. McQueen and Ernst V. West. Drawn by H. A. McQueen.

DETAIL OF ENTABLATVRE

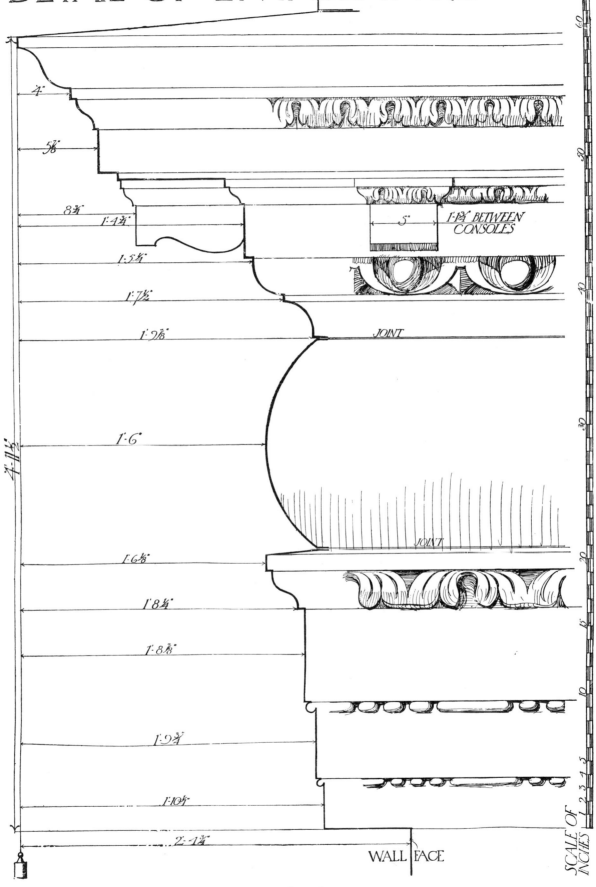

1·1¼ BETWEEN CONSOLES

5·

JOINT

JOINT

WALL FACE

SCALE OF INCHES

Nos. 57 and 58, Lincoln's Inn Fields, London.

Measured by H. A. McQueen and Ernst V. West.   Drawn by H. A. McQueen.

Plate 5

Exteriors.

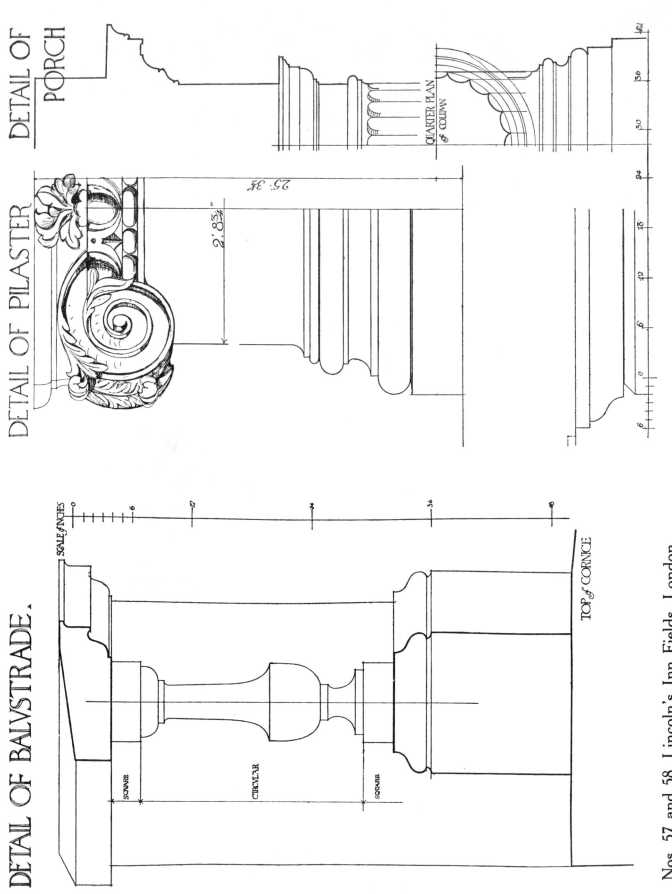

DETAIL OF PORCH

DETAIL OF PILASTER

QUARTER PLAN OF COLUMN

25′ 3⅜″

2′ 8½″

DETAIL OF BALVSTRADE.

SCALE of INCHES

SQVARE

CIRCVLAR

SQVARE

TOP of CORNICE

Nos. 57 and 58, Lincoln's Inn Fields, London.

Measured by H. A. McQueen and Ernst V. West. Drawn by H. A. McQueen.

Details of a House at Enfield, Middlesex

Plate 7   Exteriors.

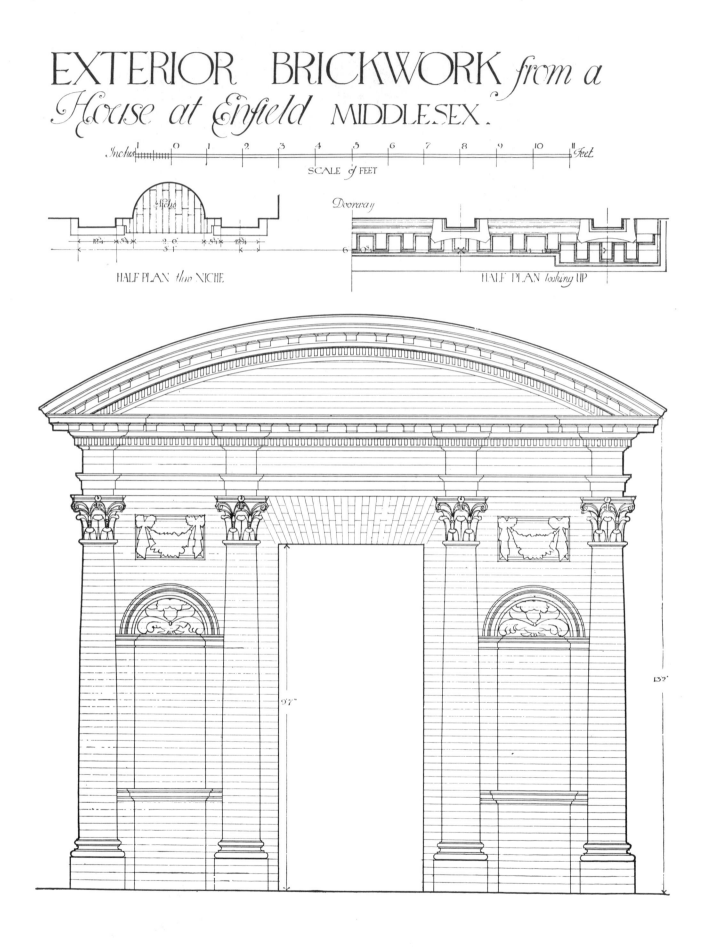

EXTERIOR BRICKWORK *from a*
House at Enfield MIDDLESEX.

SCALE of FEET

Niche

HALF PLAN *thro* NICHE

Doorway

HALF PLAN *looking* UP

Measured and Drawn by G. H. Parry and H. A. McQueen.

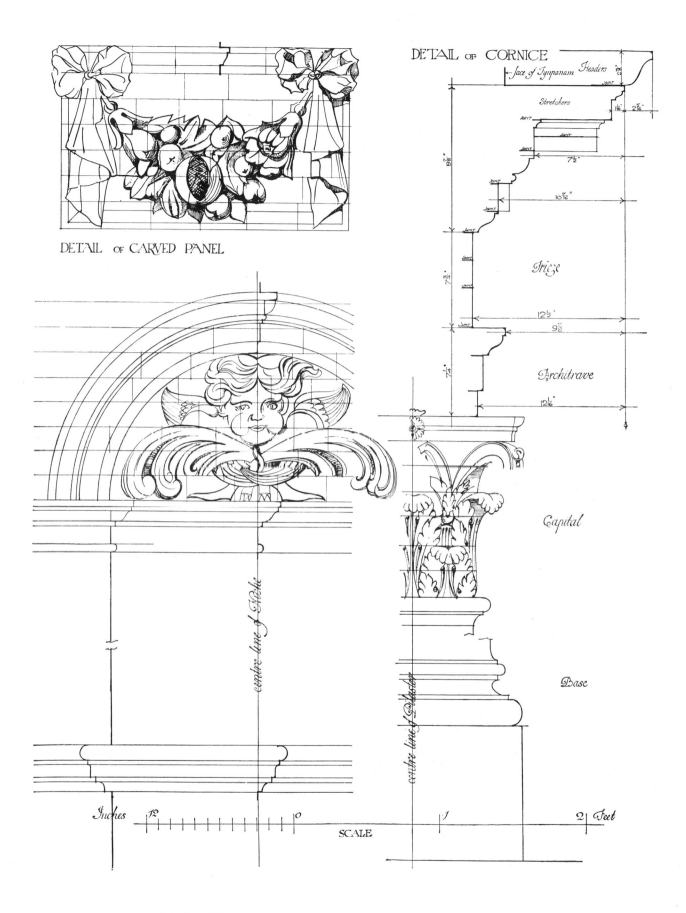

DETAIL OF CARVED PANEL

DETAIL OF CORNICE

Face of Tympanum Headers

Stretchers

Frieze

Architrave

Capital

Base

centre line of Niche

centre line of Pilaster

Inches

SCALE

Feet

Details of House at Enfield, Middlesex.

Measured and Drawn by G. H. Parry and H. A. McQueen.

Plate 9 Exteriors.

Houses in the Strand, London.

*No. 164a Strand is the right-hand one of the two
houses shown above, now demolished. (See also Plate 10)*

CONSOLE (LOOKING UP)

SKETCH

HEIGHT OF CORNICE
FROM GROUND 35'.0"

SCALE OF FEET

Wooden Cornice, No. 164a, Strand, City of Westminster

Measured and Drawn by H. A. McQueen.

Plate 11   Exteriors.

CONSOLE
(LOOKING UP)

SCALE
OF
FEET

NOTE:
ONLY MAIN LINES OF THESE
ENRICHMENTS DISCERNABLE

15½"

6¼"

5"

CENTRE LINE OF PILASTER

FACE OF WALL

SKETCH

HEIGHT OF CORNICE
FROM GROUND 36·0'

Houses in the Strand, London.   *(The cornice of another destroyed Strand building)*

Measured and Drawn by H. A. McQueen.

The School House, Risley, Derbyshire.

Plate 13   Exteriors.

The School House, Risley, Derbyshire.

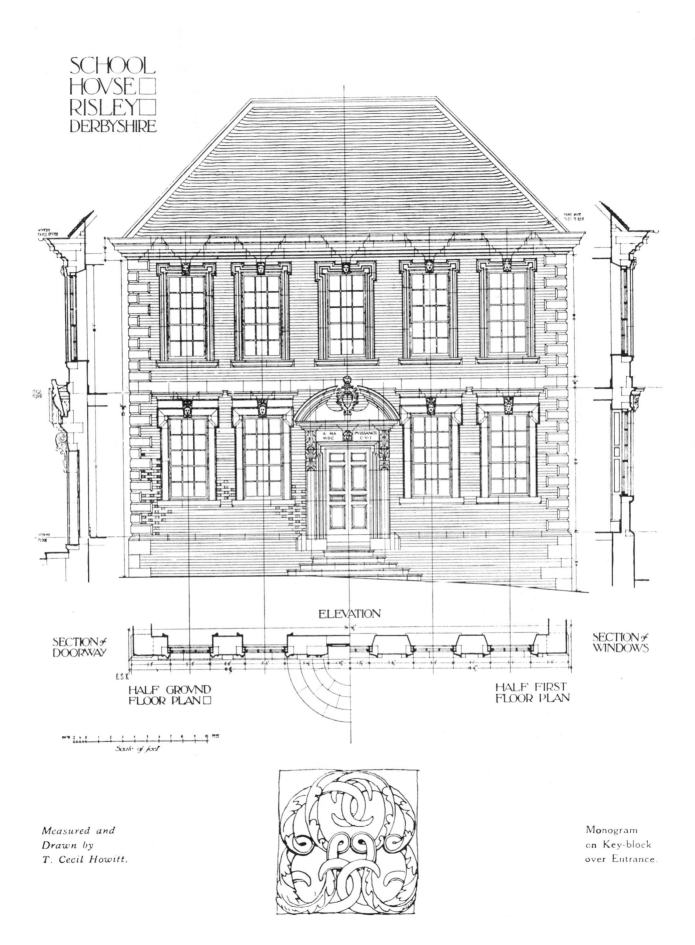

SCHOOL
HOVSE☐
RISLEY☐
DERBYSHIRE

ELEVATION

SECTION of
DOORWAY

SECTION of
WINDOWS

HALF GROVND
FLOOR PLAN☐

HALF FIRST
FLOOR PLAN

Scale of feet

*Measured and
Drawn by
T. Cecil Howitt.*

Monogram
on Key-block
over Entrance.

Plate 15   Exteriors.

SCHOOL HOVSE, RISLEY.
DOORWAY DETAILS

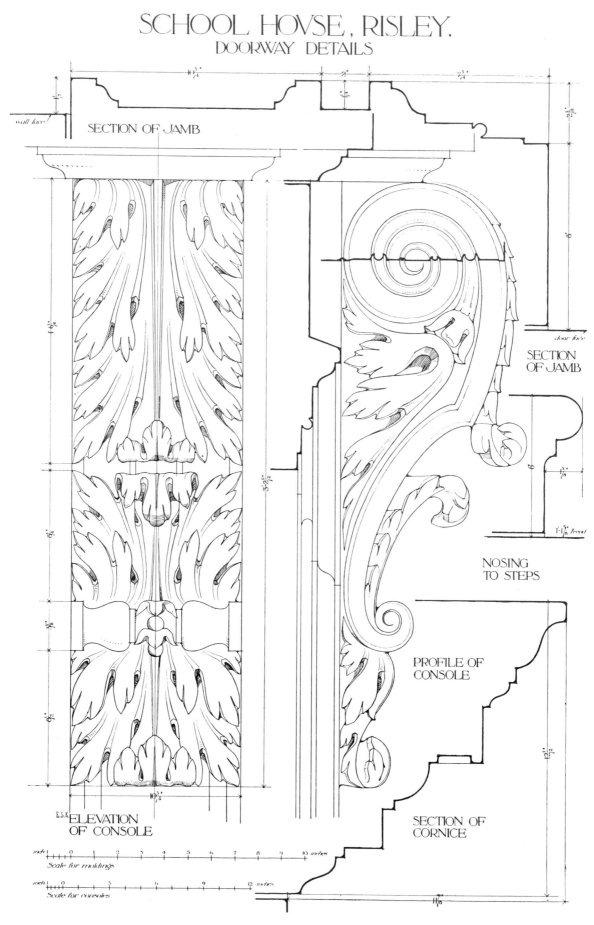

SECTION OF JAMB

SECTION OF JAMB

NOSING TO STEPS

PROFILE OF CONSOLE

ELEVATION OF CONSOLE

SECTION OF CORNICE

Scale for moldings

Scale for consoles

Measured and Drawn by T. Cecil Howitt.

SCHOOL HOVSE, RISLEY.
FRONT DETAILS

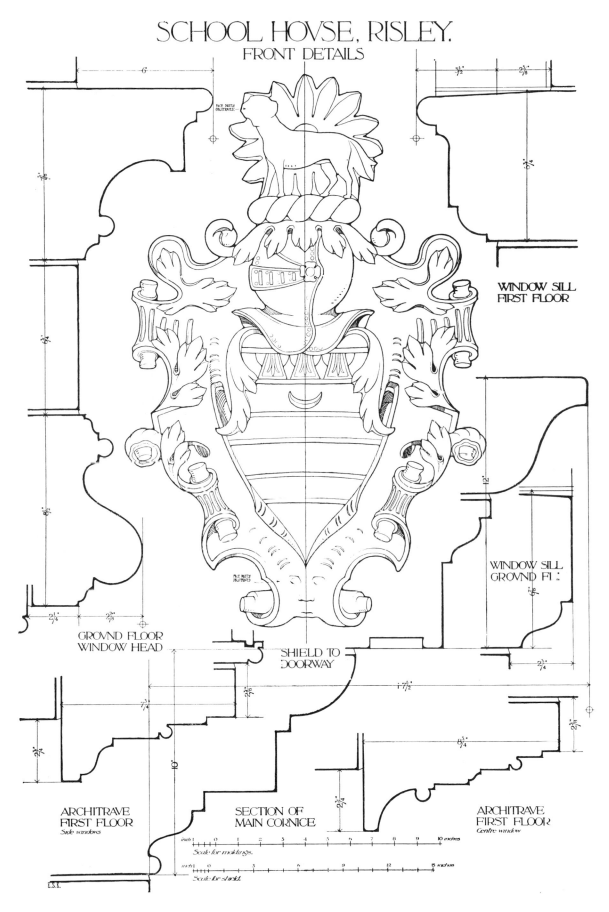

WINDOW SILL
FIRST FLOOR

WINDOW SILL
GROVND FL.

GROVND FLOOR
WINDOW HEAD

SHIELD TO
DOORWAY

ARCHITRAVE
FIRST FLOOR
Side windows

SECTION OF
MAIN CORNICE

ARCHITRAVE
FIRST FLOOR
Centre window

Scale for mouldings.

Scale for shield.

Measured and Drawn by T. Cecil Howitt.

Plate 17 Exteriors.

The Judge's Lodging, No. 16, St. Giles, Oxford.

THE JUDGES LODGING   NO 16 ST GILES OXFORD

INCHES |———————————————————————| FEET

ELEVATION

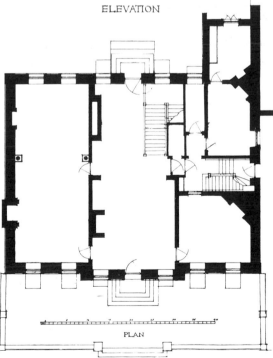

PLAN

The Front to St. Giles.

Measured and Drawn by W. R. Brinton and C. Green.

Plate 19   Exteriors.

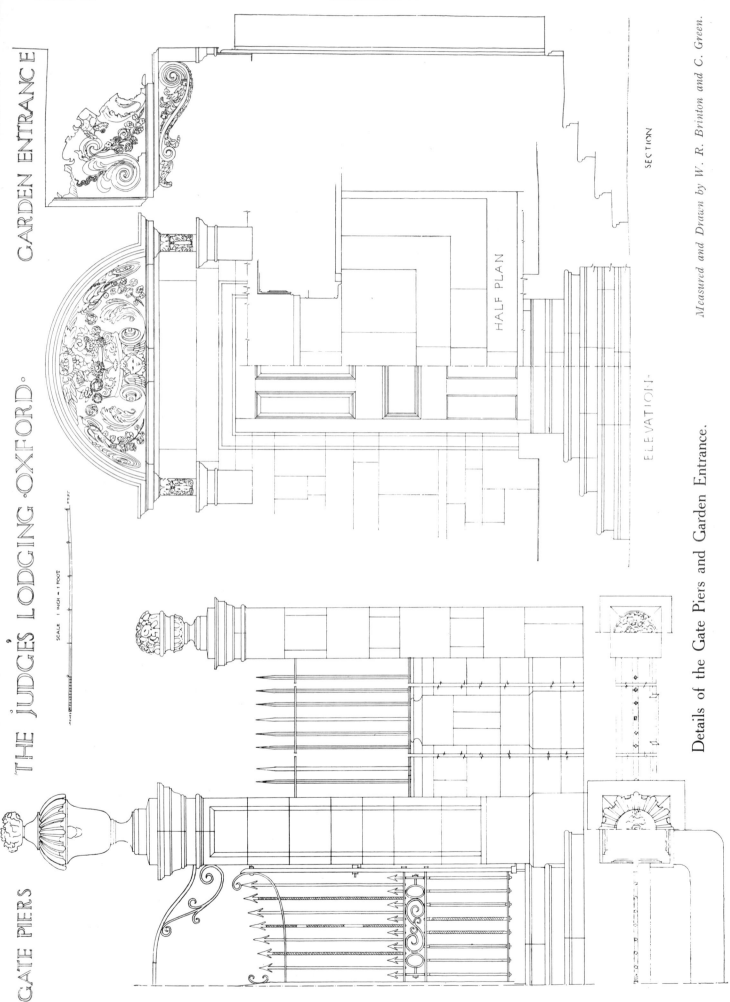

GARDEN ENTRANCE

THE JUDGES LODGING·OXFORD·

GATE PIERS

HALF PLAN

ELEVATION·

SECTION

SCALE 1 INCH = 1 FOOT

Measured and Drawn by W. R. Brinton and C. Green.

Details of the Gate Piers and Garden Entrance.

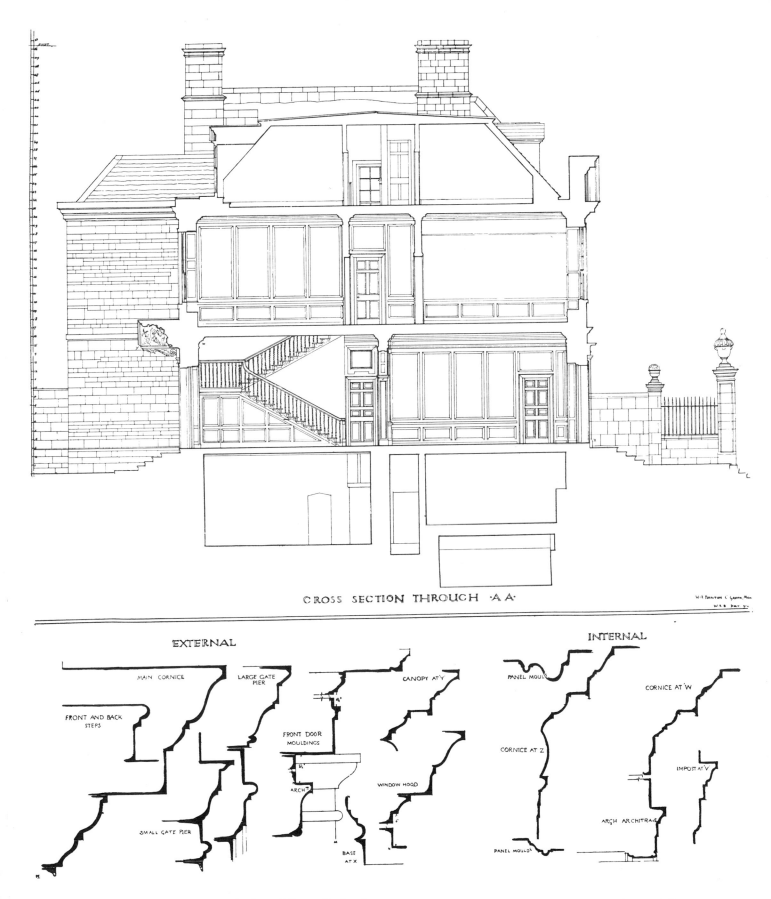

CROSS SECTION THROUGH ·A·A·

EXTERNAL

INTERNAL

MAIN CORNICE

LARGE GATE PIER

CANOPY AT 'Y'

PANEL MOUL

CORNICE AT 'W'

FRONT AND BACK STEPS

FRONT DOOR MOULDINGS

CORNICE AT Z

IMPOST AT 'V'

ARCH

WINDOW HOOD

SMALL GATE PIER

ARCH ARCHITRAVE

BASE AT X

PANEL MOULD

The Judge's Lodging, No. 16, St. Giles, Oxford.

A Section through the Centre.

Measured and Drawn
by
W. R. Brinton and C. Green.

NOTE.—*The details of mouldings are reproduced to a scale of approximately 1 inch to 1 foot.*

Plate 21   Exteriors.

Moulinière House, Wandsworth, London. (Built *circa* 1700.)

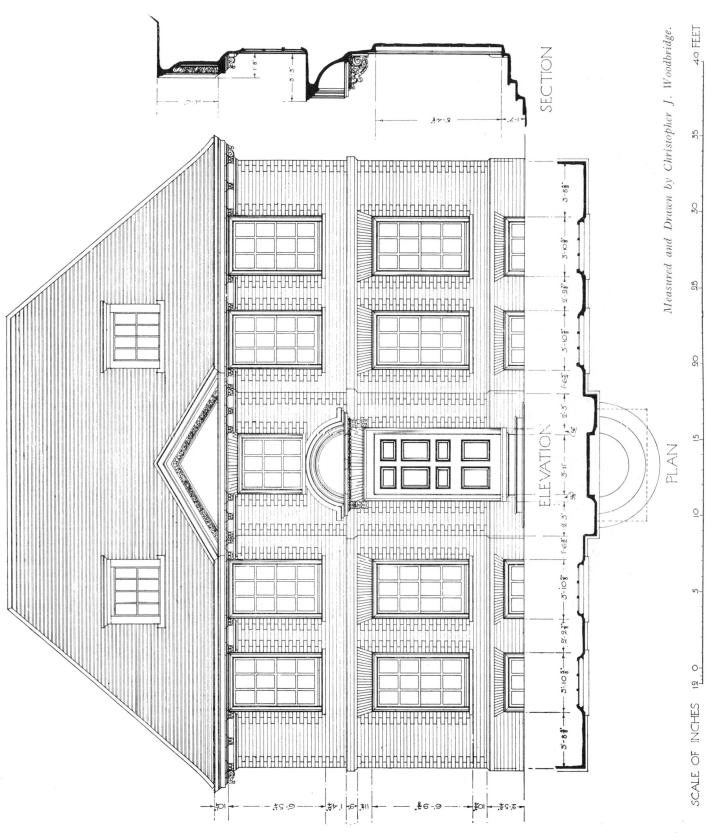

SECTION

ELEVATION

PLAN

Measured and Drawn by Christopher J. Woodbridge.

SCALE OF INCHES   12   0   5   10   15   20   25   30   35   40 FEET

Plate 23   Exteriors.

Wrencote, Croydon, Surrey.

ELEVATION

PLAN

FT. 10   5   0   10   20   30 FT.

WRENCOTE CROYDON | c 1720 | ELEVATION & PLAN

Measured and Drawn by Christopher J. Woodbridge.

Plate 25

Exteriors.

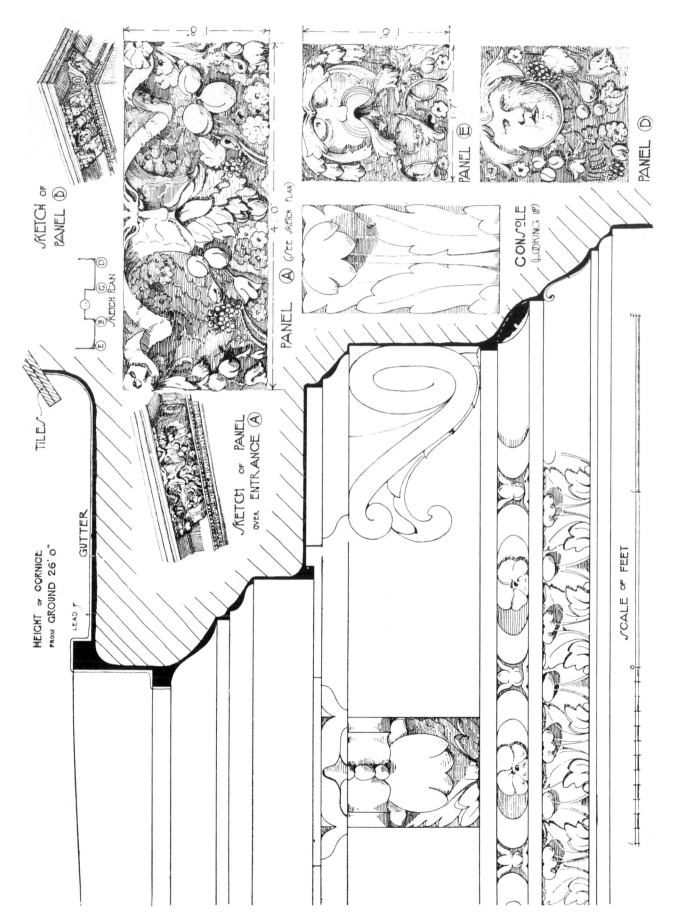

SKETCH OF PANEL D

PANEL A (SEE SKETCH PLAN)

PANEL E

PANEL D

CONSOLE (LOOKING UP)

SKETCH OF PANEL OVER ENTRANCE A

SKETCH PLAN

TILES

GUTTER

HEIGHT OF CORNICE FROM GROUND 26' 0"

LEAD

SCALE OF FEET

Wrencote, Croydon., Surrey.   Details of the Cornice.

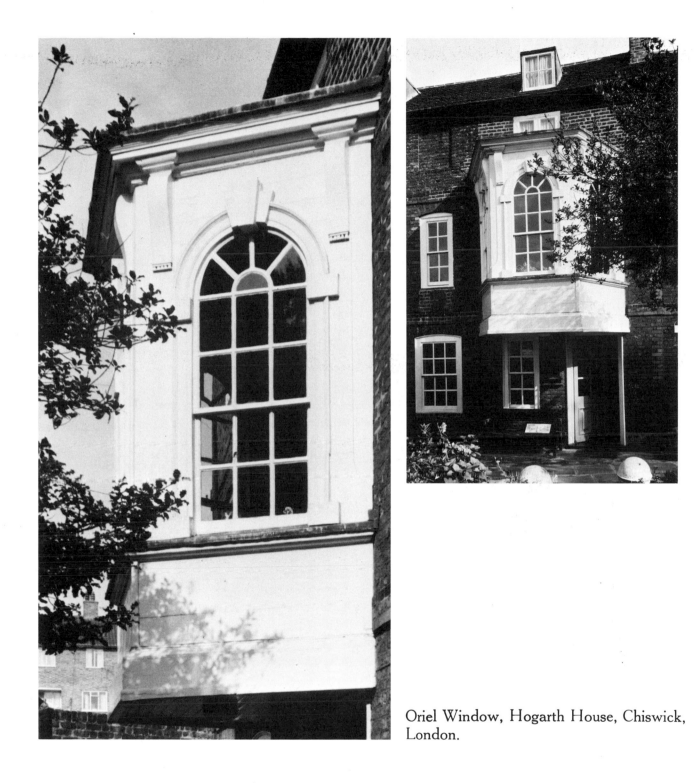

Oriel Window, Hogarth House, Chiswick, London.

Plate 27   Exteriors.

HOGARTH HOUSE.
CHISWICK.

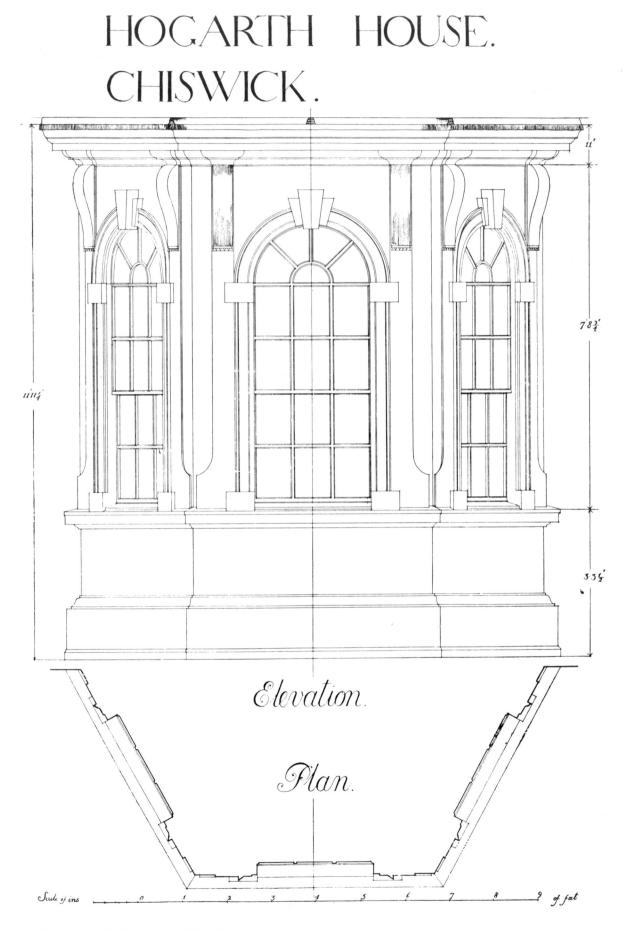

Elevation.

Plan.

Scale of ins   0   1   2   3   4   5   6   7   8   9   of feet

Measured and Drawn by B. R. Penderel-Brodhurst.

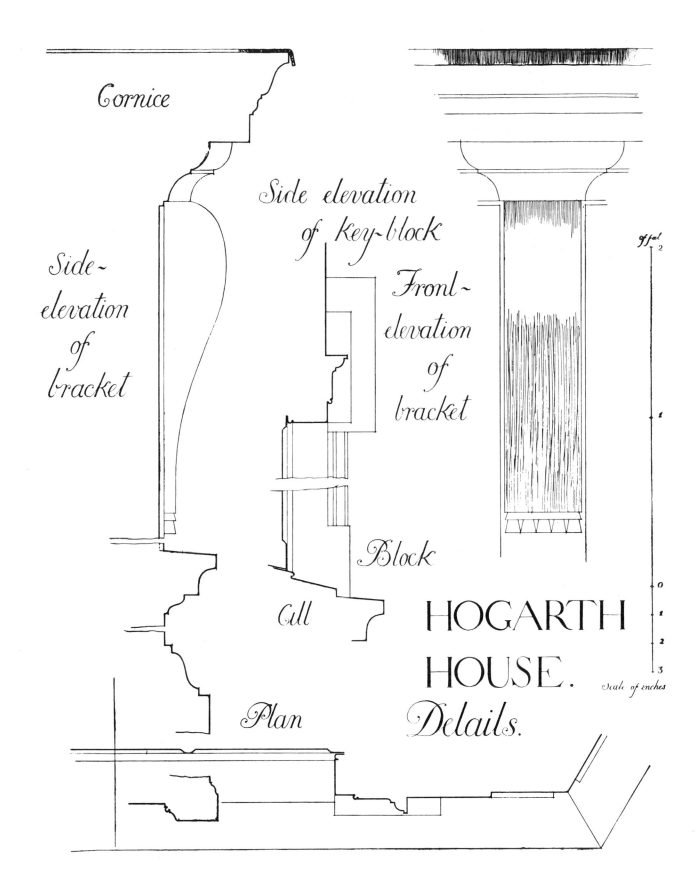

Cornice

Side elevation of bracket

Side elevation of key-block

Front elevation of bracket

Block

Sill

Plan

HOGARTH HOUSE. Details.

off ful 2
1
0
1
2
3

Scale of inches

Oriel Window, Hogarth House, Chiswick, London.

Measured and Drawn by B. R. Penderel-Brodhurst.

Plate 29

Exteriors.

Birch's, No. 15, Cornhill, London. *(This shopfront is now in the Victoria and Albert Museum)*

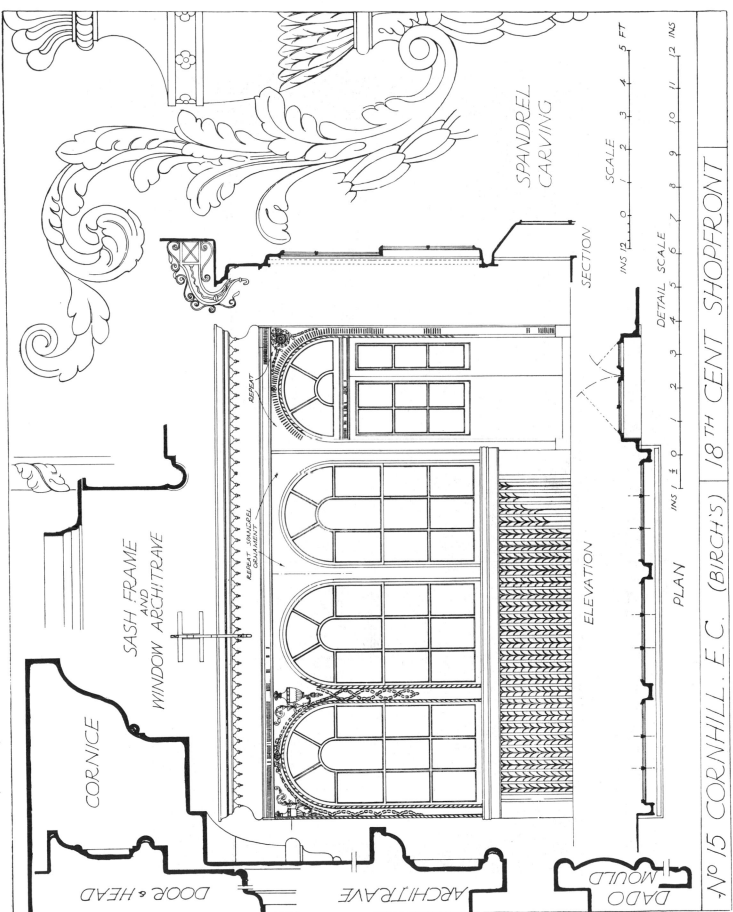

SPANDREL CARVING

SECTION

REPEAT

REPEAT SPANDREL ORNAMENT

SASH FRAME AND WINDOW ARCHITRAVE

CORNICE

ELEVATION

DOOR & HEAD

ARCHITRAVE

DADO MOULD

PLAN

DETAIL SCALE

SCALE

INS 12   5 FT   4   3   2   1   0

INS 12   11   10   9   8   7   6   5   4   3   2   1   0

INS 1   ¾   0

INS 1   ¼   0

No 15 CORNHILL. E.C. (BIRCH'S) 18TH CENT SHOPFRONT

Measured and Drawn by Christopher J. Woodbridge.

Plate 31

Exteriors.

An Eighteenth-Century Shop Front at 56, Artillery Lane, London.

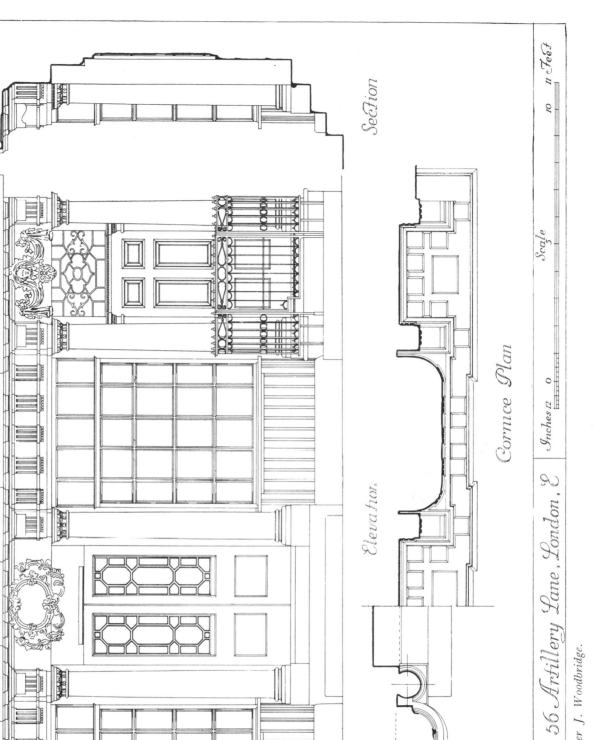

Section

Elevation

Cornice Plan

Plan

Scale

Inches 2   0   5   10   11 Feet

SHOP FRONT | 56 Artillery Lane, London, E

Measured and Drawn by Christopher J. Woodbridge.

Doorways

Notes on Plates 33—95

Plates 33–40

Nos 2, 3 and 5 King's Bench Walk, Inner Temple, London.

After a fire in the Temple in 1678, it has been suggested that Sir Christopher Wren was asked to build these three houses. Whoever the architect may have been, he showed great skill in using a simple design for them, and these doorways typify the quiet elegance of the houses. The doorway of No 5 (*Plate 38*) is the most elaborate one and uses the Corinthian order. That of No 2 (*Plate 33*) has neither capitals nor bases to the flat pilasters, and it has a very simple triangular pediment. As for No 3, even the boot-scraper is of sufficient interest to merit a drawing (*Plate 37*). Each one of these doorways is composed entirely of gauged brickwork.

Plates 41–45

Morden College, Blackheath, London.

Morden College was founded in 1695 by a rich Levant merchant, Sir John Morden, as an almshouse for persons described as 'decayed Turkey merchants'. It stands in large grounds and the main (west) front consists of a central building with wings on each side. These wings have doors with hooded porches (*Plate 41*). In the centre of the west front is the entrance doorway (*Plate 43*). A wide pediment at the top contains the statues of the founder and his wife in a double niche. Edward Strong was the master mason of Morden College but, although there is no evidence to support the fact, it is just possible that the design was by Wren. Sir Nikolaus Pevsner says it is 'indeed one of the best dozen or so of examples of Wren's style in domestic as against representational architecture'*

Plates 46–48

No 33 Mark Lane, London.

This handsome house once stood in its own grounds in Mark Lane—a street which led to the river and the Port of London and which was occupied by rich merchants who built large houses there in the seventeenth century. This, again, is one of the many houses said to have been

---

* *The Buildings of England: London (except the Cities of London and Westminster).* (Penguin Books.)

designed by Sir Christopher Wren without any evidence. Nor has it been authenticated that, as reputed, the carving on the doorway was by Grinling Gibbons. It may, however, have been the Spanish Embassy at one time. The building has been destroyed but the doorway is now on exhibition in the Victoria and Albert Museum, South Kensington.

Plates 49–52

The Judge's House (Mompesson House), The Close, Salisbury, Wiltshire.

This house is now known as 'Mompesson House,' after Charles Mompesson who built it in 1701. It has been thought to be the work of one of Wren's associates. The doorway with the window over is the main feature of the front. The pediment is filled with heraldic carving. The architrave to the door is formed of wave-moulding and is of exactly the right dimensions and in keeping with the vigorous stone detail throughout. The brackets have unusually flat scrollwork on their sides. The door and frame are of oak.

Plates 53–54

Queen Street, King's Lynn, Norfolk.

The free-standing but recessed pillars are like sticks of barley sugar. They support a pretty, sober pediment. The design is possibly by Bell of King's Lynn, the architect of that town's fine Custom House. The date is 1708 and the only pillars of similar design are in the porch of St. Mary's, Oxford.

This is the doorway to Clifton House—a famous King's Lynn building which was the home of Lynn merchants at a time when the town was one of the most flourishing ports in the country. Part of the structure of Clifton House goes back to the fourteenth century.

Plates 55–58

Formerly in Carey Street, Westminster, London.

This is an excellent example of fine seventeenth-century work. It has perfect proportions, and very stylish carving; also, the raising of the architrave to support the urn is a well contrived detail. The doorcase is now in the Victoria and Albert Museum.

Plates 59–62

House at Bocking, Essex.

This is an attractive example of an eighteenth-century shell hood. It is an addition to an older house (dated 1695) and the projecting upper storey has made it necessary to give the porch long bracket supports. The cherub heads are well carved. Although it will probably be preserved, this hood has now been dismantled, as the house to which it belonged is due for demolition.

Plates 63–64

No 12 Barnhill, Stamford, Lincolnshire.

A very striking and original late seventeenth-century doorway. The pediment has a beautiful curve and the brackets are carved with great style. The railings in front of this house are illustrated in *Plate 105*

Plates 65–66

St Anselm's, Park Lane, Croydon, Surrey.

This splendidly carved doorway belonged to a Queen Anne house, built in 1708, which used to stand in Park Lane, Croydon, until demolished by a landmine in 1940. In 1728, Sir Peter Bayliss, Lord Mayor of London, lived here, but its longest association has been with the Society of Friends who bought the house in the eighteenth century and whose meeting house now stands on the site. At the time when the plates shown here were drawn, it had been leased-out to a boys preparatory school (St Anselm's). *Plates 201–204* also show the fine panelling inside this house.

Plates 67–72

Doorways in Chelsea, London: No 2 Swan Walk; Nos 23 and 24 Lawrence Street; No 32 Cheyne Row.

The doorway of No 2 Swan Walk, as well as the two doorways which follow, date from the time when much of the open space between the ancient riverside village of Chelsea and Charles II's Hospital was used for building eighteenth-century houses. No 2 Swan Walk, with its dignified doorway, is one of the few houses of that period left in the area (*Plate 67*).

Lawrence Street and Cheyne Row have a greater number of survivors of this eighteenth-century expansion of Chelsea. The doorways of Nos 23 and 24 Lawrence Street (*Plate 69*) are early Georgian ones and are joined together under a single pediment supported by carved brackets. Both Fielding and Smollett lived in No 24. Also, John Gay wrote *The Beggar's Opera* there. Un-happily, due to a misplaced zeal to make 'improvements', the early nineteenth-century name-plate of No 24 ('Monmouth House') has now been replaced by greatly inferior lettering. No 32 Cheyne Row (*Plate 71*) belongs to a terrace of houses famous by virtue of Carlyle and others having lived in it. Its simple doorway and hood are typical features of the simple, elegant houses that were built in London in the early eighteenth century.

Plates 73–80

Doorways in The Close, Salisbury, Wiltshire.

The doorway in *Plate 73* is a good example of simple, robust Georgian work. The very effective pediment is simply ornamented with plain console blocks. The pilasters lack the usual fluting at the sides. The one in *Plate 75* has excellent detailing and carving. These two eighteenth-century doorways in the Close, Salisbury, together with the one in *Plate 78*, illustrate the variety and quality of work to be found within a small area.

Plates 81–84

Nos 16 and 17 Friar Street, Reading, Berkshire.

These doorways show the remarkably high quality of vernacular building in the eighteenth-century. This high level of design was maintained all over the country and it was supported by rigorous standards of excellence in the building trades. There is a slight divergence of style between these two examples which indicates the joiner's skill. He probably owed a lot to copy-books, like Batty Langley's, but he brought to his work a certain traditional scholarship that gave him freedom to avoid exact imitations of his model without losing anything of its character. This is why there are countless doorways all over the country that conform to a few definite types, yet hardly two are exactly alike.

Nos 16 and 17 Friar Street have been demolished and a block of offices now stands on the site.

Plates 85–86

Doorway in Rodney Street, Liverpool.

Rodney Street, Liverpool, is in the Georgian area of the city and consists of a row of brick houses, all built in the late-eighteenth and early-nineteenth centuries. It contains many pleasant front doorways which usually have well detailed Ionic or Doric columns. The doorway illustrated here is recessed and has Doric columns and lintel and a large, finely detailed fanlight over the door.

Plates 87–88

Balbardie House, Bathgate, West Lothian.
This porch is one of a pair on the north front of this Robert Adam house, designed in 1792. They are really alcoves of very striking design, reminiscent of the apse or tribune of the Roman basilicae. The alcove is crossed at the springing height of the enclosing arch by a light, fluted entablature supported on elegant columns. The entablature is surmounted by a vase and, above the arch, there is a deep frieze with finely carved festoons. Adam used this kind of alcove composition most often indoors (e.g. the library at Kenwood, Hampstead), and it probably derives from The Temple of Jupiter at Spalato, in Dalmatia, which he carefully measured in 1764.

Plates 89–92

East Borough, Wimborne, Dorset.
The porch and railings are both eighteenth-century work, but the porch was crudely repaired at a later date, as can be seen in *Plate 89* (top illustration). A slight extra projection of the porch's centre pillars allows the entablature to be returned, also giving the pediment a little extra prominence. The railings are very ingenious and unlike the usual work of this period (*Plate 92*).
In *Plate 89*, the top view shows how the house looked many years ago, and the view below shows how it looks today—an example of how a well-built house can remain as up-to-date as ever if well looked after. Unfortunately, the railings have now gone, but the pediment of the porch appears to be, once again, as first designed and as originally drawn (see *Plate 90*).

Plates 93–95

House at Wimborne, Dorset.
A good standard type of Georgian door. The brackets, placed clear of the architrave on a slight plain pilaster, carry the pediment. The carved frieze is of poor quality but it contributes a pleasing richness. The standards finishing the railing are cast—a good example of the skilful way the smiths of the eighteenth century combined wrought-iron with cast-iron. Unfortunately, the stone casing and pediment have been allowed to decay and have lately had to be dismantled.

Plate 33

Doorways.

No. 2, King's Bench Walk, Temple, London.

Nº 2 KING'S BENCH WALK, E.C.

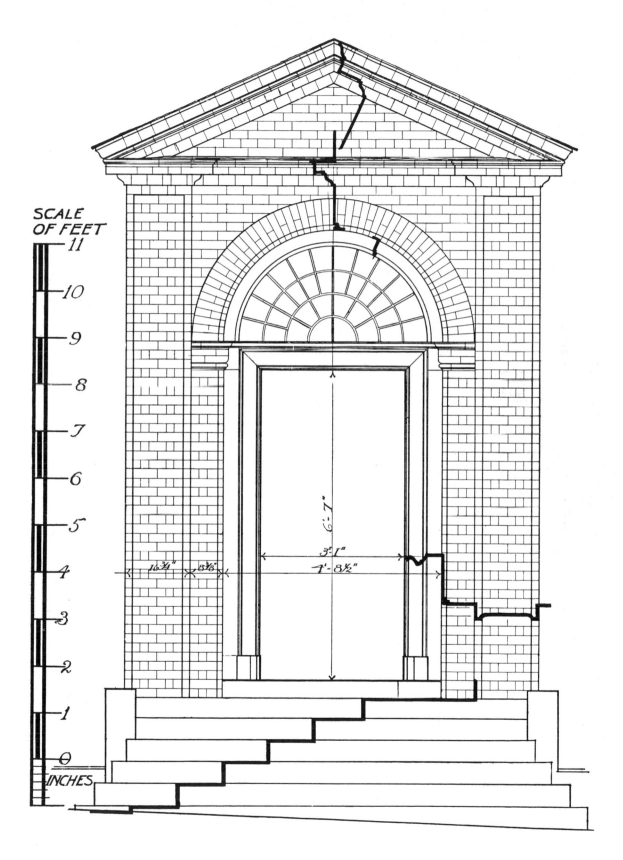

Measured and Drawn by Ernst V. West.

Plate 35

Doorways.

No. 3, King's Bench Walk, Temple, London.

Nº 3 KING'S BENCH WALK, E.C.

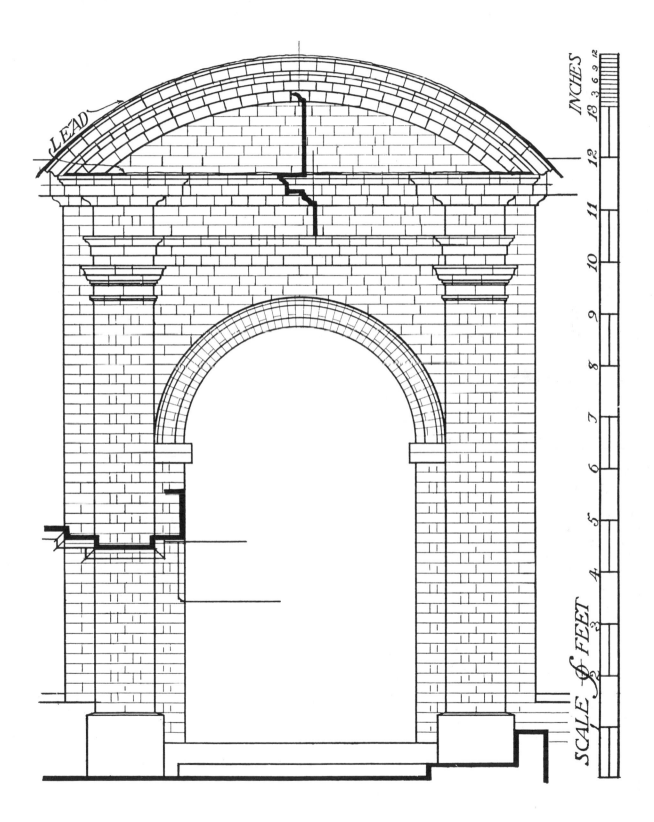

Measured and Drawn by Ernst V. West.

Plate 37

Doorways.

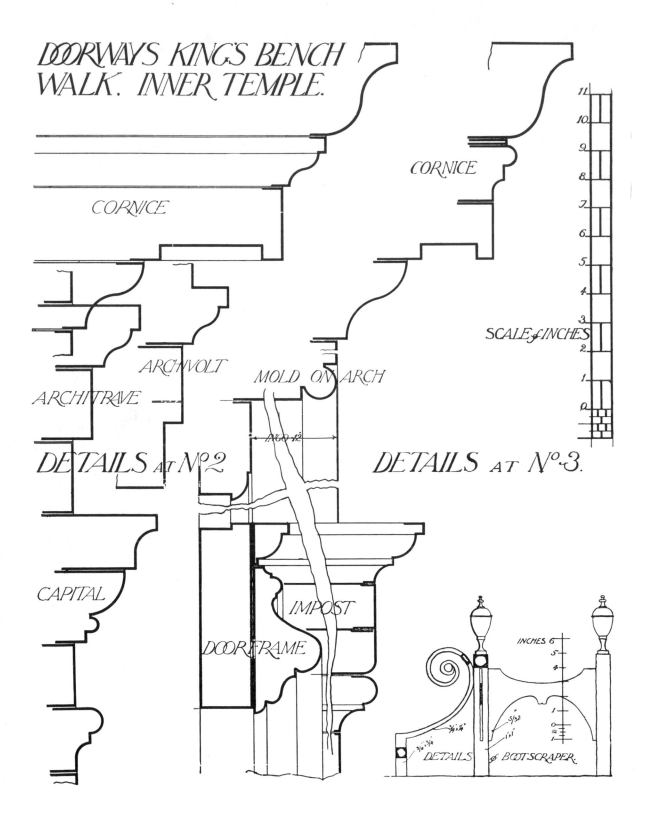

DOORWAYS KING'S BENCH WALK. INNER TEMPLE.

CORNICE

CORNICE

ARCHVOLT

ARCHITRAVE

MOLD ON ARCH

SCALE OF INCHES

DETAILS AT Nº 2.

DETAILS AT Nº 3.

CAPITAL

IMPOST

DOOR FRAME

INCHES

DETAILS OF BOOT SCRAPER.

Measured and Drawn by Ernst V. West.

Doorway, No. 5, King's Bench Walk, Temple, London.

Plate 39

Doorways.

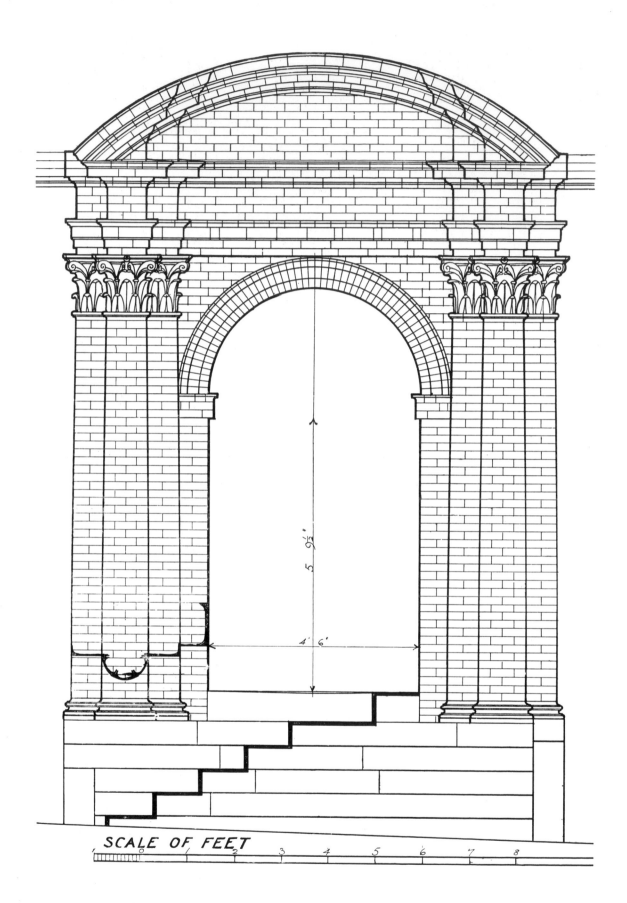

SCALE OF FEET

1 0 1 2 3 4 5 6 7 8

Doorway, No. 5, King's Bench Walk, Temple, London.

Measured and Drawn by Ernst V. West.

DETAIL OF CORNICE

SCALE OF FEET

ARCHITRAVE

LEAD

ARCHIVOLT

STONE CAP.

DETAILS OF·DOOR-WAY, INN-ER·TEMPLE

HALF PLAN OF CAP LOOKING UP

STONE BASE

No. 5, King's Bench Walk, Temple, London.

Measured and Drawn by Ernst V. West.

Plate 41

Doorways.

Morden College, Blackheath, Kent, England.   Details of Doorway to South Wing.

Measured and Drawn by T. Frank Green.   *Details of Door Measured by A. J. Healey, and Drawn by A. Bough.*

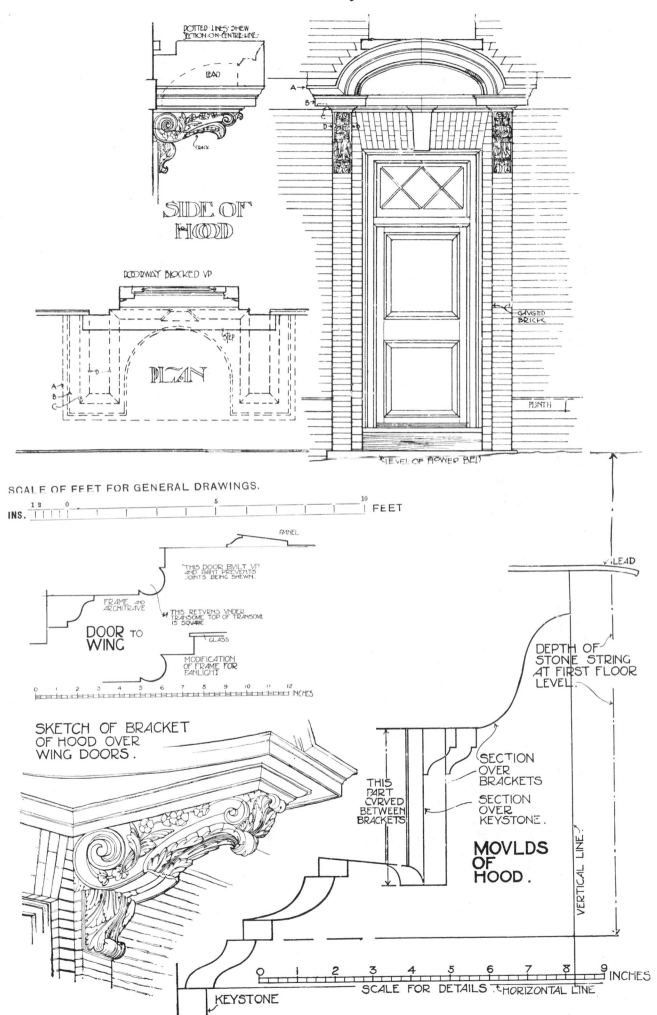

DOTTED LINES SHEW
SECTION ON CENTRE LINE.

LEAD

CRACK

SIDE OF
HOOD

DOORWAY BLOCKED VP

A
B
C
D

STEP

PLAN

GAVGED
BRICK

PLINTH

LEVEL OF FLOWER BED

SCALE OF FEET FOR GENERAL DRAWINGS.

1 2   0   5   10
INS.   FEET

PANEL

THIS DOOR BVILT VP
AND PAINT PREVENTS
JOINTS BEING SHEWN.

FRAME AND
ARCHITRAVE

THIS RETVRNS VNDER
TRANSOME TOP OF TRANSOME
IS SQUARE.

DOOR TO
WING

GLASS

MODIFICATION
OF FRAME FOR
FANLIGHT.

0 1 2 3 4 5 6 7 8 9 10 11 12 INCHES

LEAD

SKETCH OF BRACKET
OF HOOD OVER
WING DOORS.

DEPTH OF
STONE STRING
AT FIRST FLOOR
LEVEL.

SECTION
OVER
BRACKETS

SECTION
OVER
KEYSTONE.

THIS
PART
CVRVED
BETWEEN
BRACKETS

MOVLDS
OF
HOOD.

VERTICAL LINE.

KEYSTONE

0 1 2 3 4 5 6 7 8 9 INCHES

SCALE FOR DETAILS. HORIZONTAL LINE.

Plate 43

Doorways.

Morden College, Blackheath, Kent, England.   Main Doorway.

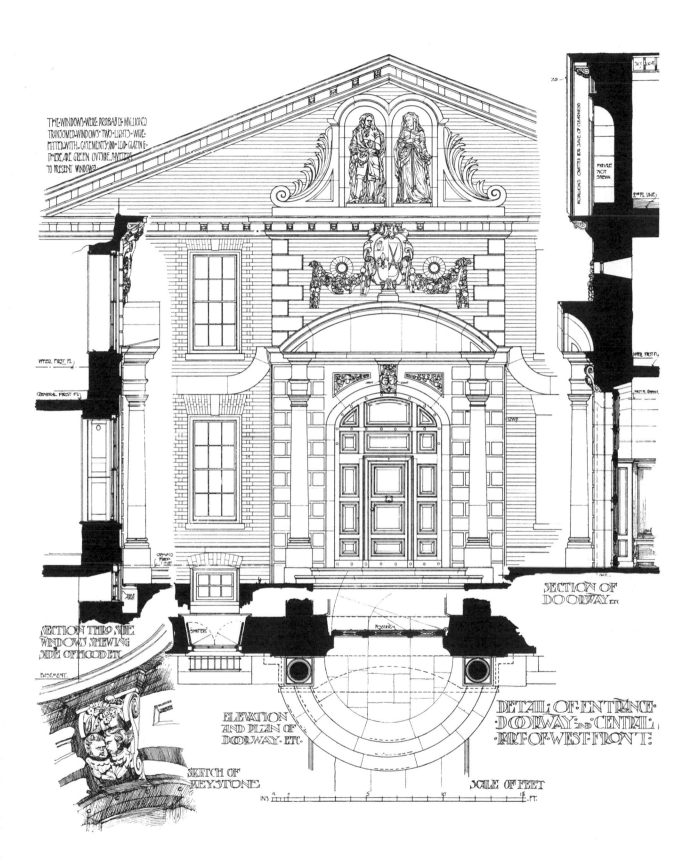

THE·WINDOWS·WERE·PROBABLY·MULLIONED
TRANSOMED·WINDOWS·TWO·LIGHTS·WIDE·
FITTED·WITH·CASEMENTS·AND·LEAD·GLAZING·
THESE·ARE·GREEN·OUTSIDE·SHUTTERS·
TO·PRESENT·WINDOWS·

SECTION OF
DOORWAY ETC

SECTION·THRO·SIDE·
WINDOWS·SHEWING·
SIDE·OF·HOOD·ETC·

ELEVATION
AND·PLAN·OF·
DOORWAY·ETC·

DETAIL·OF·ENTRANCE·
DOORWAY·AND·CENTRAL·
PART·OF·WEST·FRONT·

SKETCH·OF·
KEYSTONE

SCALE·OF·FEET

Morden College, Blackheath, Kent, England.   Details of Main Doorway.

Measured and Drawn by T. Frank Green.   Details of Door Measured by A. J. Healey, and Drawn by A. Bough.

Plate 45

Doorways.

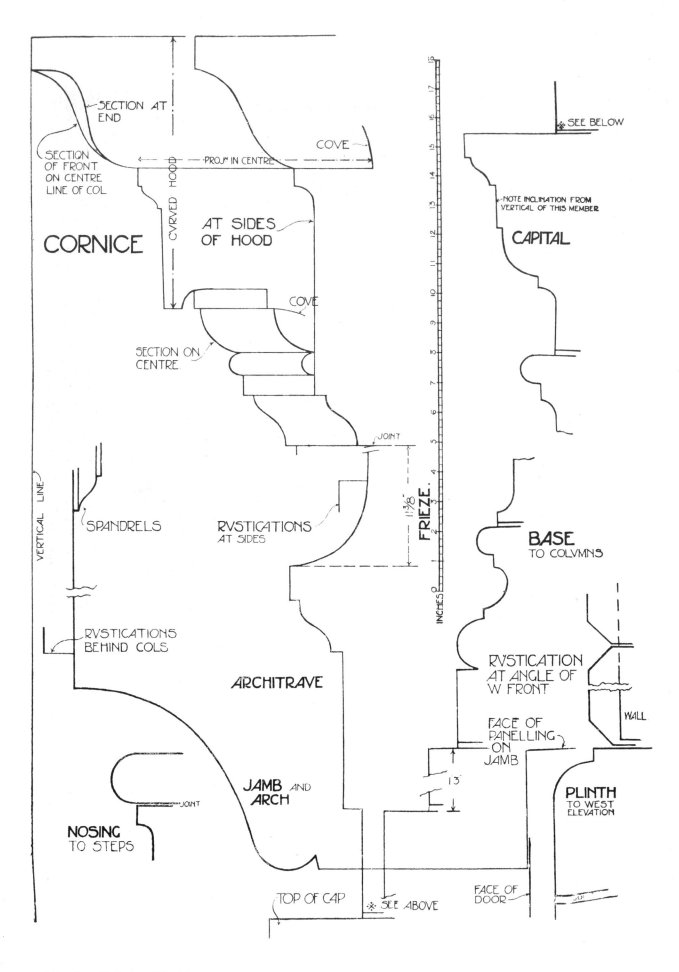

SECTION AT END

SECTION OF FRONT ON CENTRE LINE OF COL

CORNICE

PROJ^N IN CENTRE

CVRVED HOOD

COVE

AT SIDES OF HOOD

COVE

SECTION ON CENTRE

JOINT

CAPITAL

NOTE INCLINATION FROM VERTICAL OF THIS MEMBER

SEE BELOW

FRIEZE.

1·3/8"

INCHES

VERTICAL LINE

SPANDRELS

RVSTICATIONS AT SIDES

BASE TO COLVMNS

RVSTICATIONS BEHIND COLS

ARCHITRAVE

RVSTICATION AT ANGLE OF W FRONT

FACE OF PANELLING ON JAMB

WALL

JAMB AND ARCH

JOINT

NOSING TO STEPS

13

PLINTH TO WEST ELEVATION

TOP OF CAP

SEE ABOVE

FACE OF DOOR

Morden College, Blackheath, Kent, England   Details of Main Doorway.

Measured and Drawn by T. Frank Green.

The Spanish Embassy, 1680, 33, Mark Lane, London.

Plate 47   Doorways.

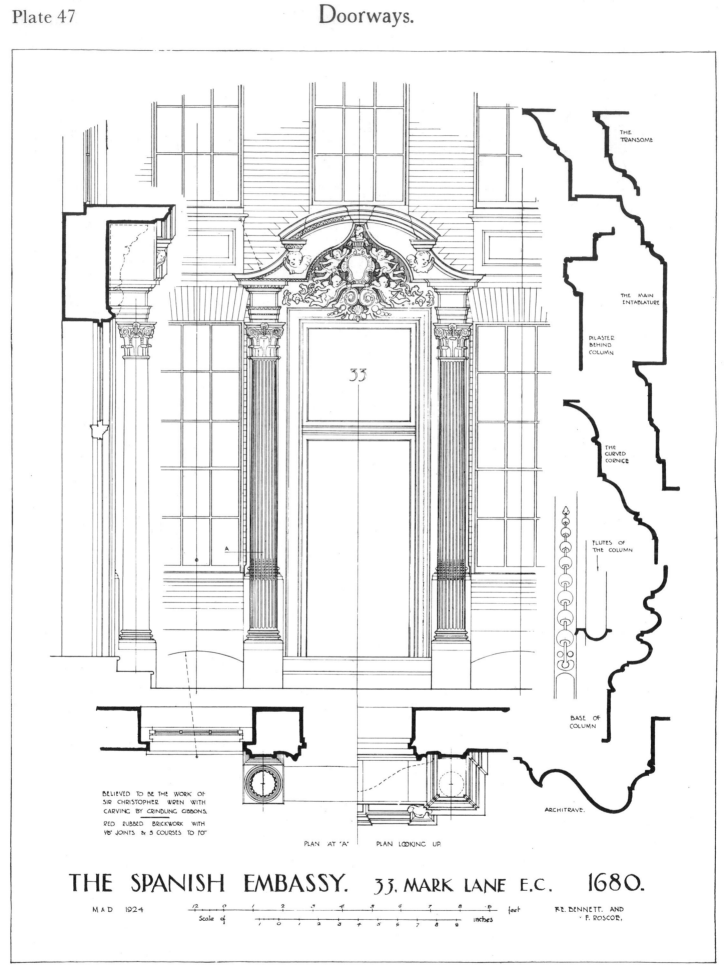

THE SPANISH EMBASSY. 33. MARK LANE E.C. 1680.

M & D 1924   Scale of   feet   inches   F.E. BENNETT. AND F. ROSCOE.

Measured and Drawn by F. E. Bennett and F. Roscoe.

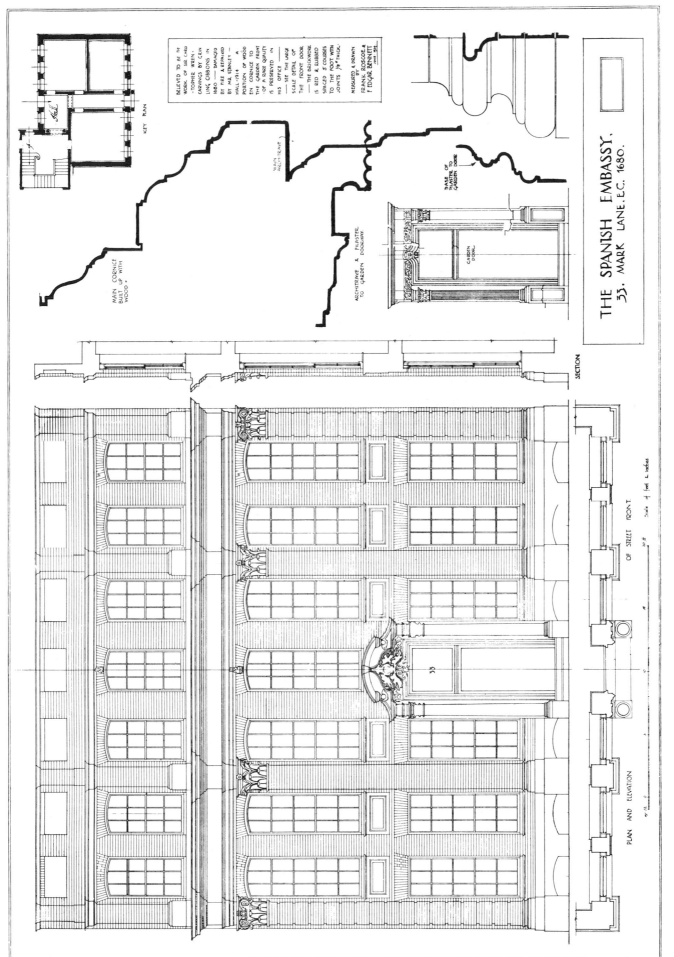

THE SPANISH EMBASSY. 33. MARK LANE. E.C. 1680.

BELIEVED TO BE TH
WORK OF SIR CHRIS
-TOPHER WREN.
CARVINGS BY GRIN
LING GIBBONS IN
1680 — DAMAGED
BY FIRE & REPAIRED
BY MR. STANLEY —
HALL.1914 — A
PORTION OF WOOD
EN CORNICE TO
THE GARDEN FRONT
-OF A RARE QUALITY
IS PRESERVED IN
HIS OFFICE
— SEE THE LARGE
SCALE DETAIL OF
THE FRONT DOOR
— THE BRICKWORK
IS RED & RUBBED
SPACED 5 COURSES
TO THE FOOT WITH
JOINTS 1/16" THICK.

MEASURED & DRAWN
BY
FRANK ROSCOE &
F. EDGAR BENNETT
JUNE 1914

MAIN CORNICE
BUILT UP WITH
WOOD.

KEY PLAN

MAIN ARCHITRAVE

ARCHITRAVE & PILASTER
TO GARDEN DOORWAY

BASE OF
PILASTER TO
GARDEN DOOR

GARDEN DOOR.

SECTION

PLAN AND ELEVATION

OF STREET FRONT

Scale of feet & inches

Measured and Drawn by F. E. Bennett and F. Roscoe.

Plate 49   Doorways.

Doorway, "The Judge's House," The Close, Salisbury.

SCALE OF FEET.

0   5   10   15

Doorway, "The Judge's House," The Close, Salisbury.

Measured and Drawn by the late J. M. W. Halley, and H. A. McQueen.

Plate 51

Doorways.

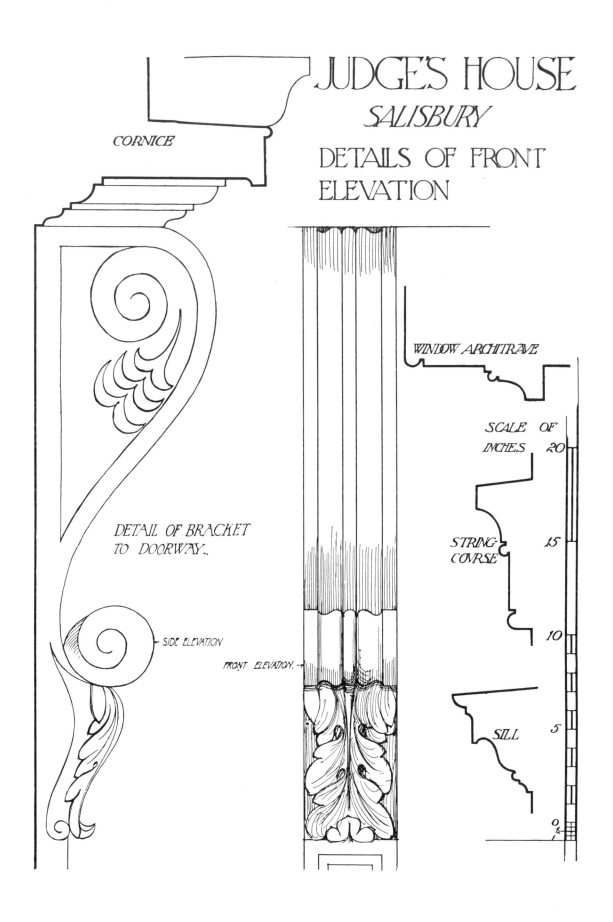

JUDGE'S HOUSE
SALISBURY
DETAILS OF FRONT
ELEVATION

CORNICE

WINDOW ARCHITRAVE

SCALE OF
INCHES   20

DETAIL OF BRACKET
TO DOORWAY.

STRING-
COURSE   15

SIDE ELEVATION

10

FRONT ELEVATION.

SILL   5

0
4

Measured and Drawn by the late J. M. W. Halley, and H. A. McQueen.

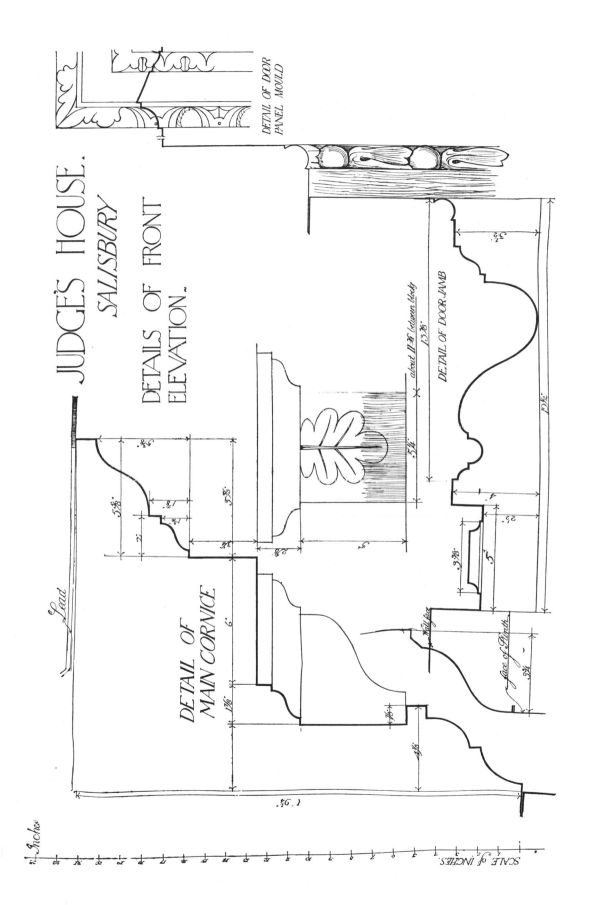

JUDGE'S HOUSE. SALISBURY

DETAILS OF FRONT ELEVATION.

DETAIL OF DOOR PANEL MOULD

DETAIL OF MAIN CORNICE

DETAIL OF DOOR JAMB

Measured and Drawn by the late J. M. W. Halley, and H. A. McQueen.

Plate 53

Doorways.

Doorway in Queen Street, King's Lynn, Norfolk.

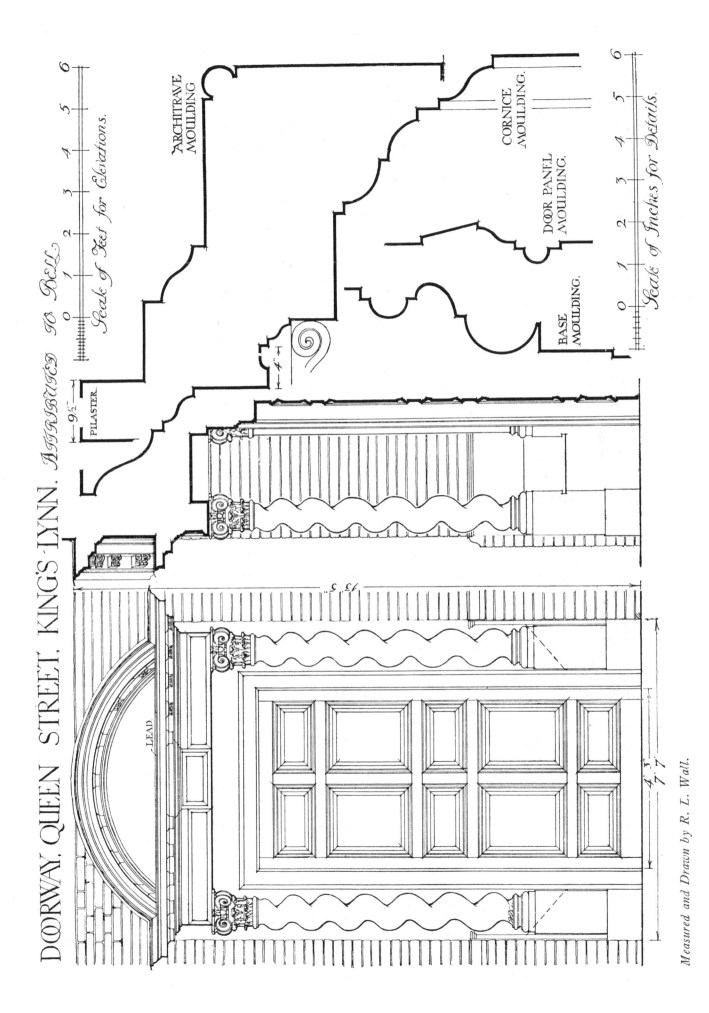

DOORWAY, QUEEN STREET, KING'S LYNN. *ASCRIBED TO BELL.*

Scale of Feet for Elevations.

Scale of Inches for Details.

ARCHITRAVE MOULDING.

CORNICE MOULDING.

DOOR PANEL MOULDING.

BASE MOULDING.

PILASTER.

LEAD.

Measured and Drawn by R. L. Wall.

Plate 55 Doorways.

Doorway removed from a House in Carey Street, City of Westminster, England.
Now in the Victoria and Albert Museum, South Kensington, London.

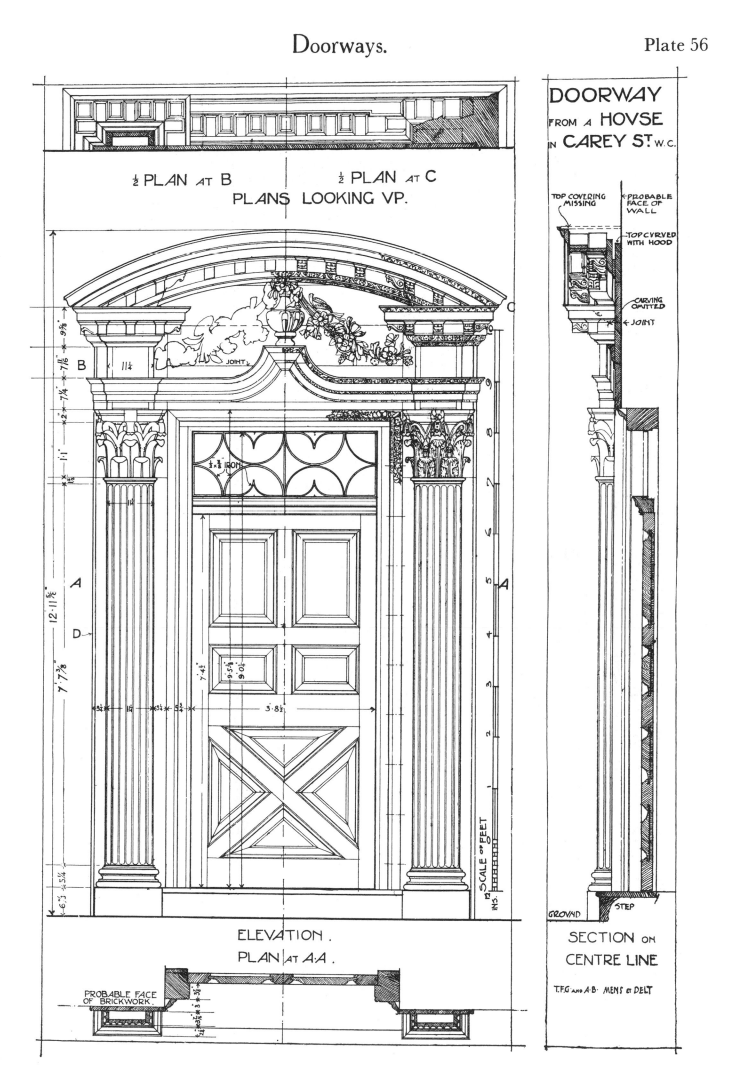

½ PLAN AT B ½ PLAN AT C

PLANS LOOKING VP.

DOORWAY
FROM A HOVSE
IN CAREY ST. W.C.

TOP COVERING MISSING

PROBABLE FACE OF WALL

TOP CVRVED WITH HOOD

CARVING OMITTED

JOINT

JOINT

SCALE OF FEET

INS.

ELEVATION.

PLAN AT A·A.

PROBABLE FACE OF BRICKWORK

SECTION ON CENTRE LINE

GROVND

STEP

T.F.G AND A·B· MENS ET DELT

Plate 57   Doorways.

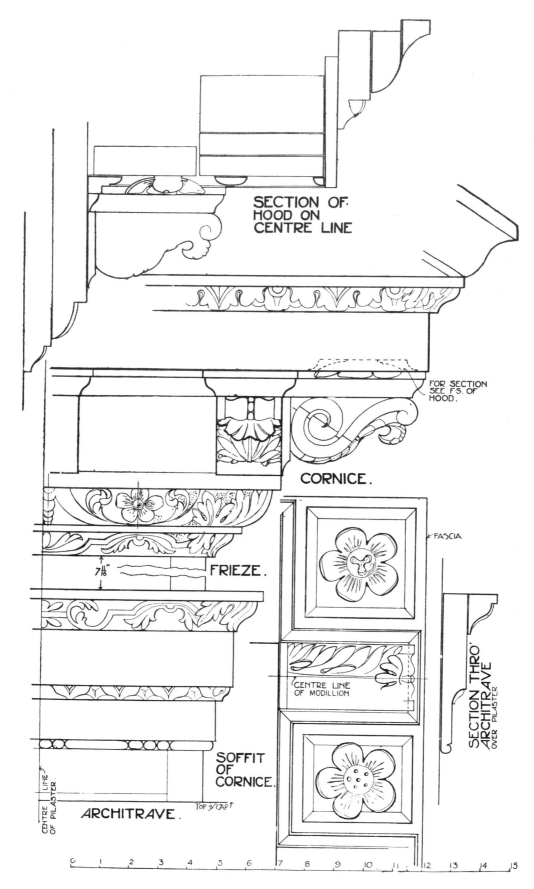

SECTION OF.
HOOD ON
CENTRE LINE

FOR SECTION
SEE F.S. OF
HOOD.

CORNICE.

FASCIA

FRIEZE.

7 11/16"

CENTRE LINE
OF MODILLION

SECTION THRO'
ARCHITRAVE
OVER PILASTER

SOFFIT
OF
CORNICE.

CENTRE LINE
OF PILASTER

ARCHITRAVE.

TOP OF CAP.T

0 1 2 3 4 5 6 7 8 9 10 11 12 13 14 15

Doorway in the Victoria and Albert Museum, removed from a House in
Carey Street, City of Westminster

Measured and Drawn by T. Frank Green.

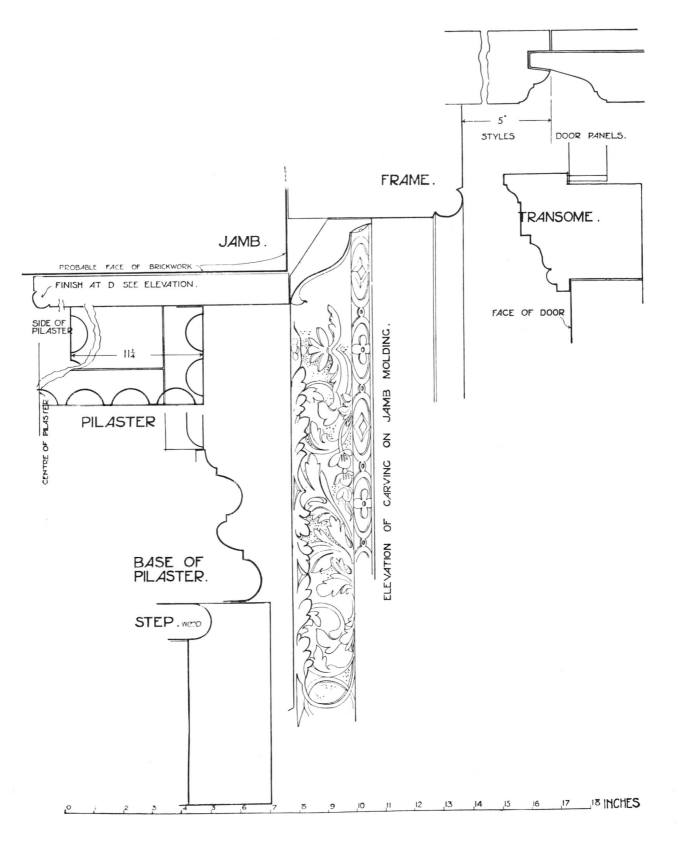

STYLES

DOOR PANELS.

FRAME.

TRANSOME.

FACE OF DOOR

JAMB.

PROBABLE FACE OF BRICKWORK

FINISH AT D SEE ELEVATION.

SIDE OF
PILASTER

11¼

CENTRE OF PILASTER

PILASTER

ELEVATION OF CARVING ON JAMB MOLDING.

BASE OF
PILASTER.

STEP. WOOD

0 1 2 3 4 5 6 7 8 9 10 11 12 13 14 15 16 17 18 INCHES

Doorway in the Victoria and Albert Museum, removed from a House in Carey Street,
City of Westminster

Measured and Drawn by T. Frank Green.

Plate 59

Doorways.

Doorway, Bocking High Street, Essex.

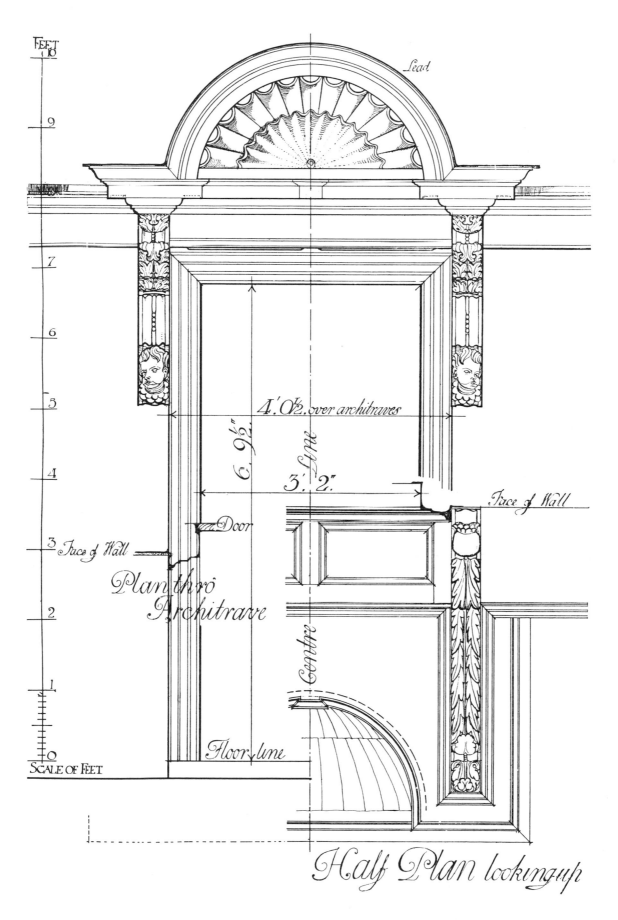

FEET
10
9
7
6
5
4
3 — Face of Wall
2
1
0
SCALE OF FEET

Lead

4'.0½". over architraves

6. 9½"

3'. 2".

Line

Centre

Face of Wall

Door

Plan thro'
Architrave

Floor line

Half Plan looking up

Doorway, Bocking High Street, Essex.

Measured and Drawn by H. A. McQueen.

Plate 61   Doorways.

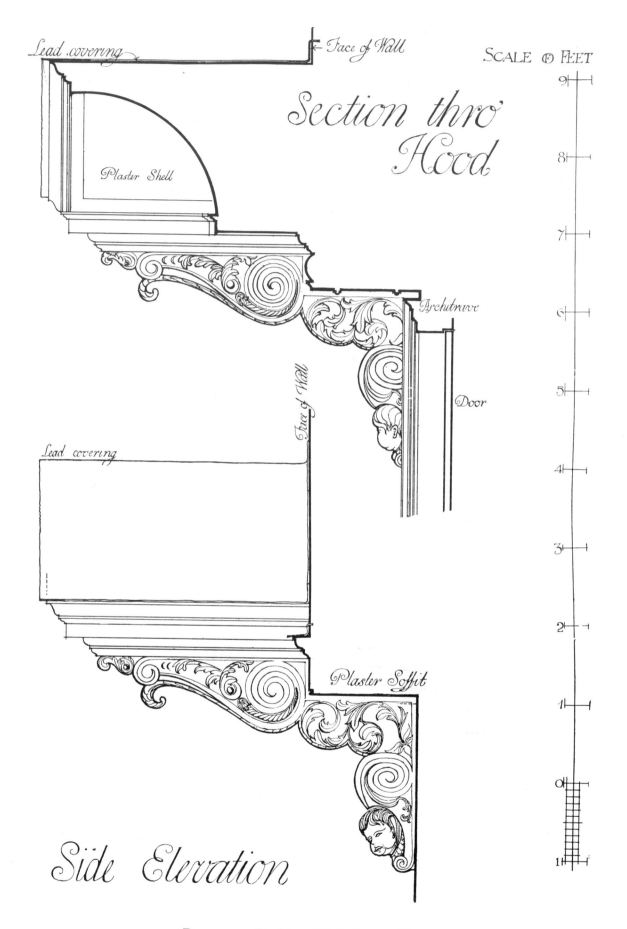

Lead covering

Face of Wall

SCALE ⊕ FEET

Section thro' Hood

Plaster Shell

Architrave

Door

Lead covering

Face of Wall

Plaster Soffit

Side Elevation

Doorway, Bocking High Street, Essex.

Measured and Drawn by H. A. McQueen.

DETAILS Doorway
Bocking High St
ESSEX

Face of Plaster

Lead

SIDE OF BRACKET

4'·2"

Measured and Drawn by H. A. McQueen.

Plate 63

Doorways.

Doorway, No. 12, Barnhill, Stamford, Lincolnshire.

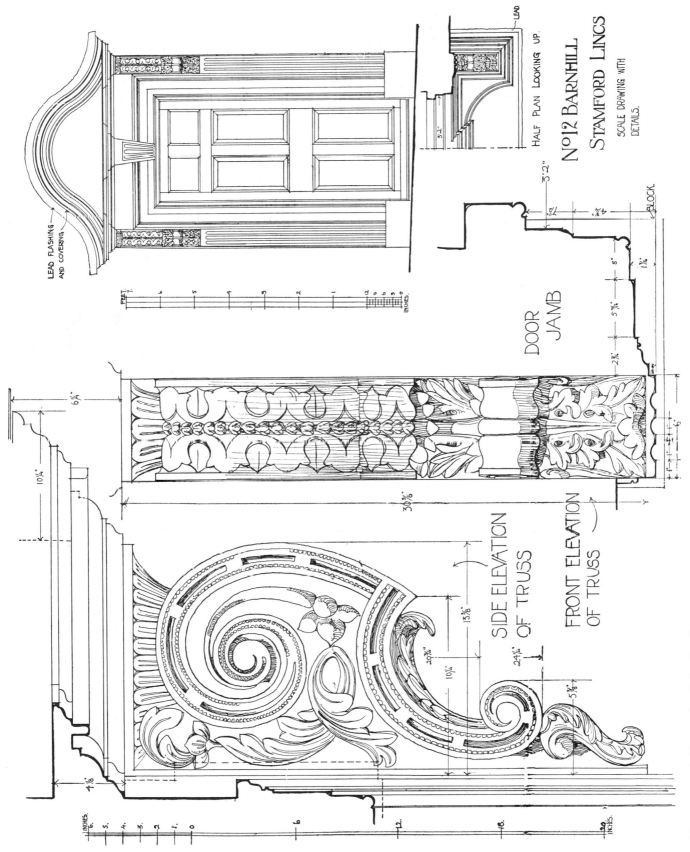

LEAD FLASHING AND COVERING

LEAD

HALF PLAN LOOKING UP.

Nº 12 BARNHILL STAMFORD LINCS

SCALE DRAWING WITH DETAILS.

BLOCK

DOOR JAMB

SIDE ELEVATION OF TRUSS

FRONT ELEVATION OF TRUSS

Measured and Drawn by John B. Lawson.

Plate 65

Doorways.

The Front Door, St. Anselm's Preparatory School, Croydon, Surrey.

CORNICE

ARCHITRAVE

BASE

ELEVATION

HALF PLAN

SECTION

CARVING
DETAIL

DETAILS SCALE

12 INS

6

0

SCALE OF FEET

15 FT   12 INS

10

5

FEET   0

DOORCASE *FROM ST. ANSELM'S SCHOOL CROYDON.* 18TH. CENT.

Measured and Drawn by Christopher J. Woodbridge.

Plate 67

Doorways.

No. 2, Swan Walk, Chelsea, London.

The Front Door and Doorcase (in carved oak).

ELEVATION

SECTION

SCALE FOR DETAILS

INS. 1 ½ 0 1 2 3 4 5 6 7

DOOR ARCHITRAVE

DETAIL OF CORNICE

SOFFIT PANEL
DOTTED

AREA

DETAIL
OF
ARCHITRAVE

DETAIL
OF BASE

DOOR

PANEL
MOULD

HALF PLAN

DOORCASE (CARVED OAK)

N° 2 SWAN WALK
CHELSEA

SCALE

INS 6 3 0 1 2 3 FT

Measured and Drawn by Christopher J. Woodbridge.

Plate 69   Doorways.

A Double Doorway in Lawrence Street, Cheyne Row, Chelsea.

CORNICE

CARVED
BRACKET

ARCHITRAVE

CAP

GLASS
LINE

DOOR
HEAD

GLASS

C

A   A

B   B

ELEVATION

GLASS
LINE

SECTION
C-C

DOOR PANEL
MOULD

PLAN
AT A-A

PLAN LOOKING
UP AT B-B

SECTION D-D

SCALE
INS 12 6 0   1   2   3   4   5 FEET.

DETAIL SCALE
INS 0 1   5   10 INS

ENTRANCE DOORS | LAWRENCE STREET
CHEYNE ROW   CHELSEA. | SEVENTEENTH
CENTURY

Measured and Drawn by Christopher J. Woodbridge.

Plate 71

Doorways.

The Front Doorway of 32, Cheyne Row, Chelsea, London.

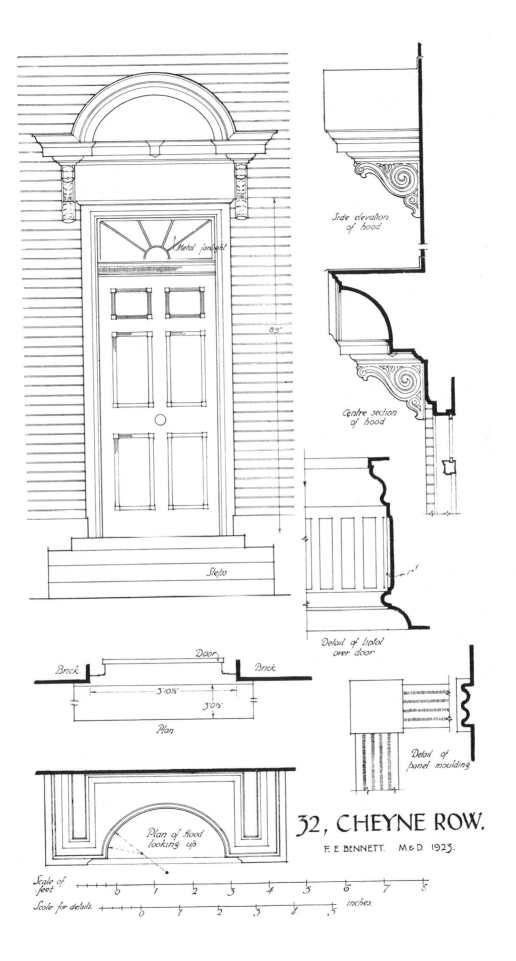

Metal fanlight

8'9"

Steps

Side elevation of hood

Centre section of hood

Detail of lintol over door

Brick.   Door   Brick

3'10½"

3'0½"

Plan

Detail of panel moulding

Plan of Hood looking up

32, CHEYNE ROW.

F. E. BENNETT.   M. & D.   1923.

Scale of feet
0 1 2 3 4 5 6 7 8

Scale for details.
0 1 2 3 4 5   inches.

Measured and Drawn by F. E. Bennett.

Plate 73   Doorways.

Doorway in the Close, Salisbury.

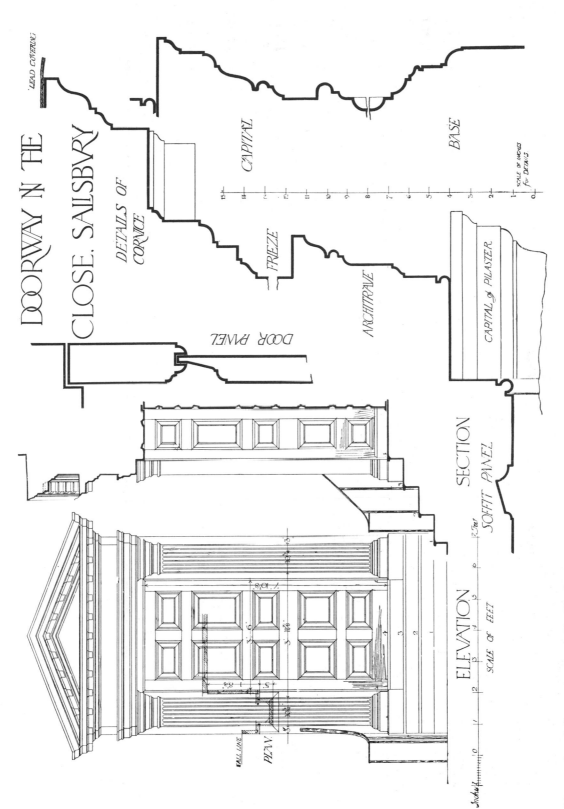

DOORWAY IN THE CLOSE. SALISBVRY

DETAILS OF CORNICE

LEAD COVERING

CAPITAL

FRIEZE

ARCHITRAVE

BASE

SCALE OF INCHES FOR DETAILS

DOOR PANEL

CAPITAL of PILASTER

SOFFIT PANEL

SECTION

ELEVATION

PLAN

WALL LINE

SCALE OF FEET

Measured and Drawn by Ernst V. West.

Plate 75

Doorways.

From the Close, Salisbury.

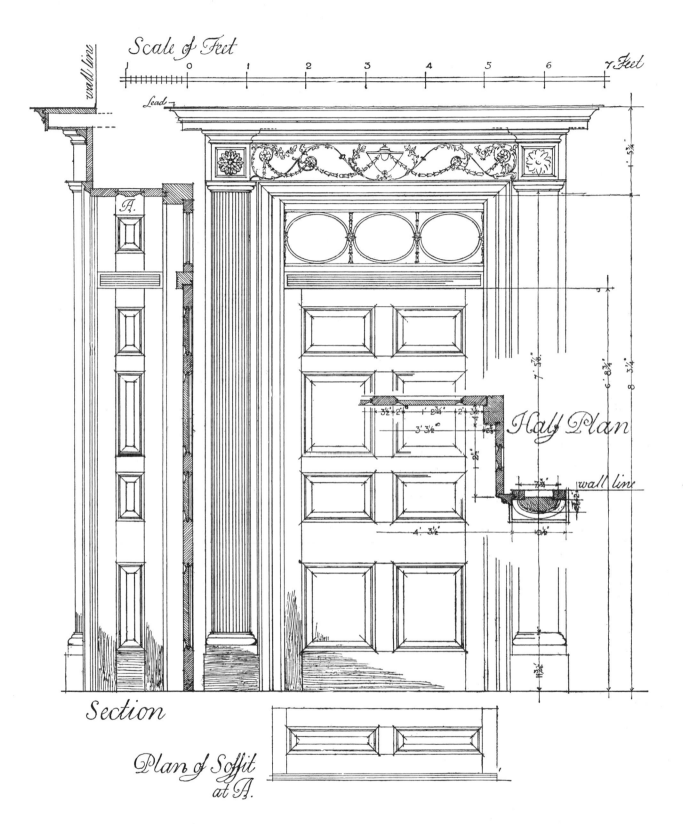

Scale of Feet

Section

Plan of Soffit
at A.

Half Plan

Measured and Drawn by H. A. McQueen.

Plate 77   Doorways.

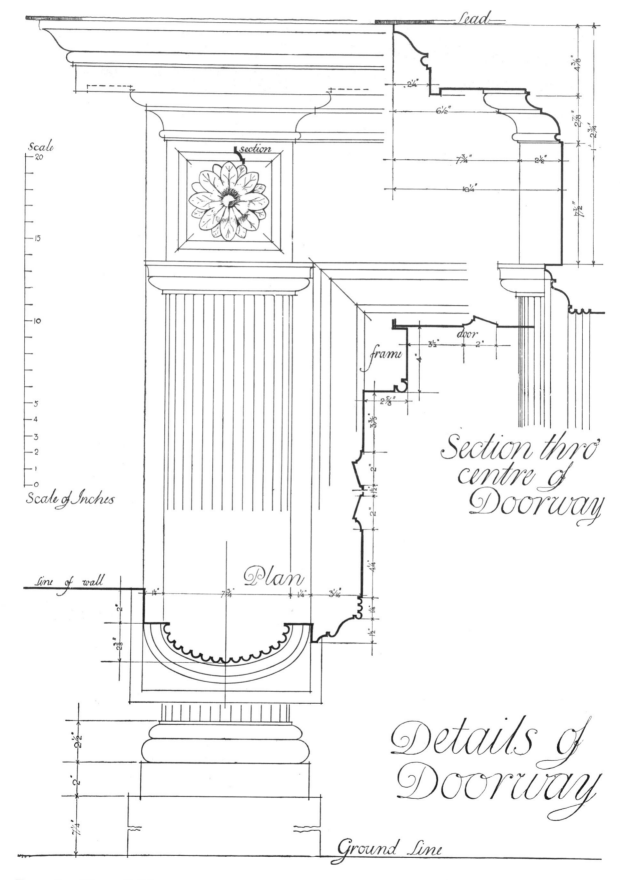

Lead

Scale
20

15

10

5
4
3
2
1
0

Scale of Inches

section

frame

door

Section thro'
centre of
Doorway

Plan

Line of wall

Details of
Doorway

Ground Line

From the Close, Salisbury.

Measured and Drawn by H. A. McQueen.

From the Close, Salisbury.

Plate 79

Doorways.

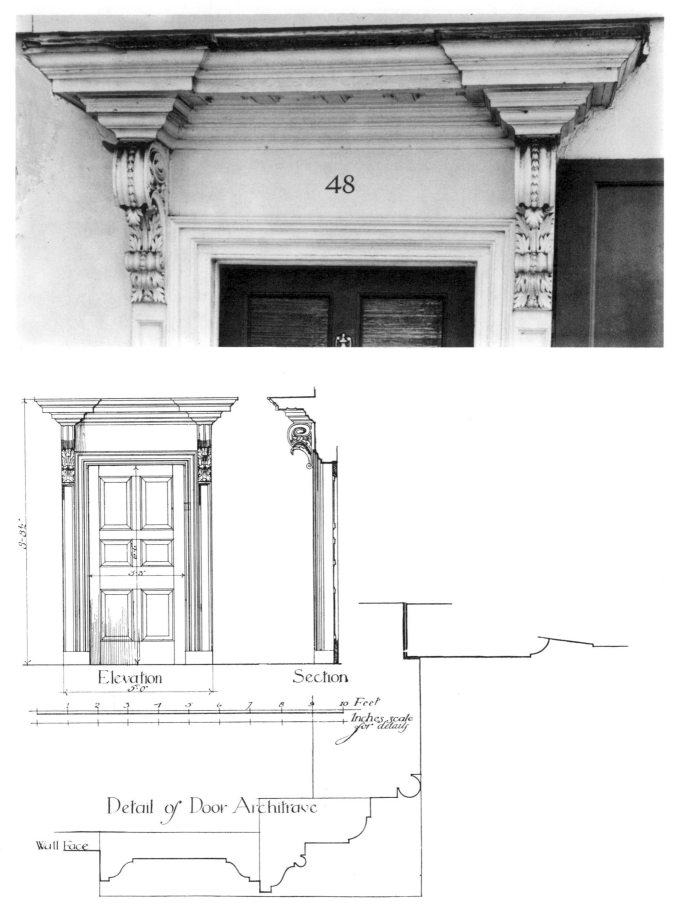

48

Elevation

5'0"

Section

1 2 3 4 5 6 7 8 9 10 Feet

Inches scale
for details

Detail of Door Architrave

Wall Face

From the Close, Salisbury.

Measured and Drawn by J. M. W. Halley.

DETAILS OF DOORWAY

SIDE OF TRUSS

FRONT OF TRUSS

1-6.

10¼

5¼

5¼

Measured and Drawn by J. M. W. Halley.

Plate 81   Doorways.

16 Friar Street, Reading.

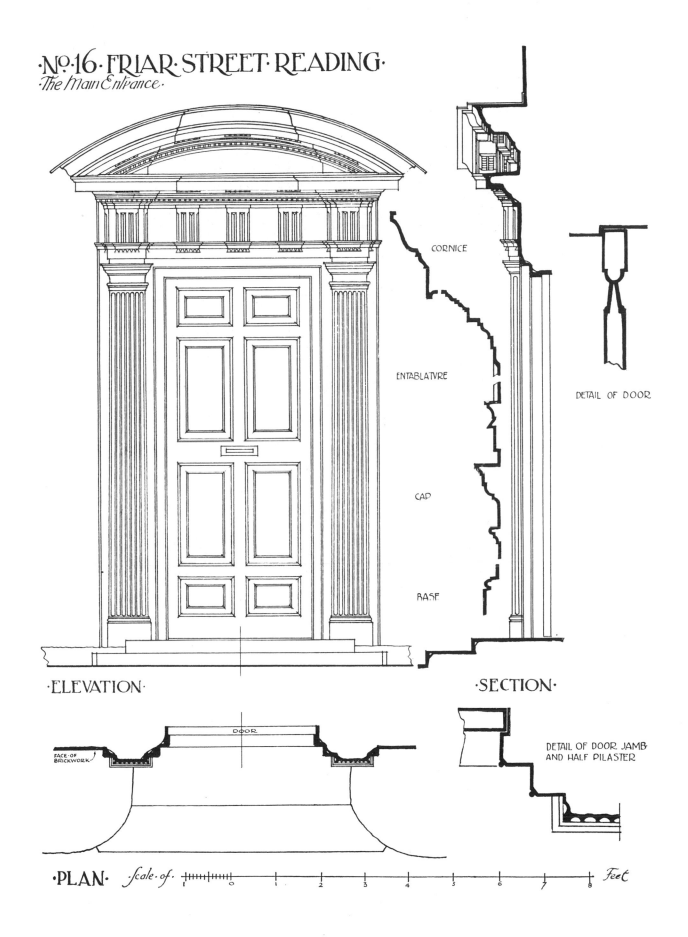

·N⁰·16·FRIAR·STREET·READING·
·The Main Entrance·

CORNICE

ENTABLATVRE

CAP

BASE

DETAIL OF DOOR

·ELEVATION·

·SECTION·

FACE·OF
BRICKWORK

DOOR

DETAIL OF DOOR JAMB
AND HALF PILASTER

·PLAN· scale of · 0 1 2 3 4 5 6 7 8 Feet

Measured and Drawn by Jasper P. Salwey, A.R.I.B.A.

Plate 83

Doorways.

17, Friar Street, Reading.

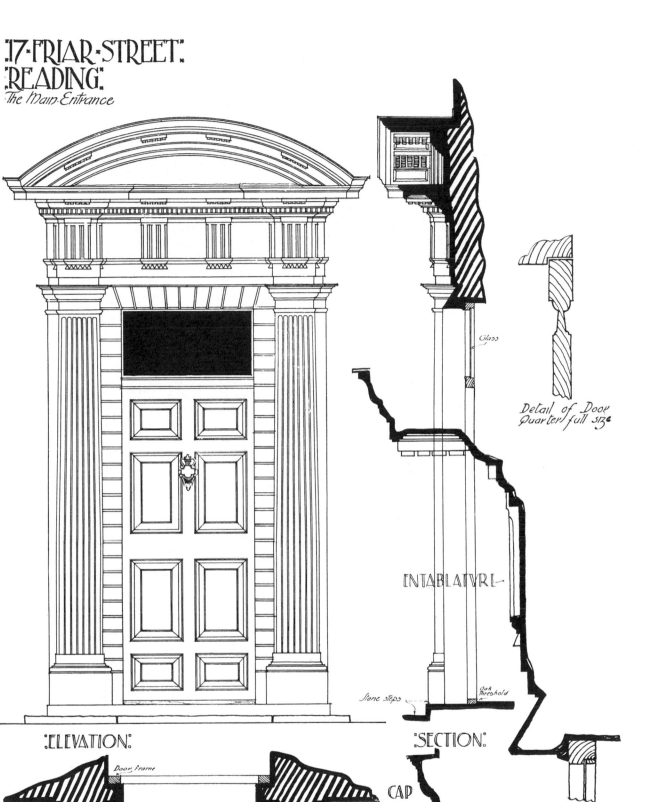

.17.FRIAR.STREET.
.READING.
The Main Entrance

Glass

Detail of Door
Quarter full size

ENTABLATVRE

Stone steps

Oak threshold

.ELEVATION.

.SECTION.

Door frame

CAP

.PLAN.

BASE

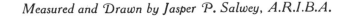

scale ⊢ 6ʹ 0 1 2 3 4 5 6 7 8 9 10 of feet

Measured and Drawn by Jasper P. Salwey, A.R.I.B.A.

Plate 85

Doorways.

A Georgian Doorway in Rodney Street, Liverpool.

·GEORGIAN DOORWAY·RODNEY ST, LIVERPOOL·

Sheet No. 4.

·Elevation·

·Plan·

Scale 1 Inch to 1 Foot

Measured and drawn by:-
R. H. Graddon · April 1923.

Measured and Drawn by R. H. Graddon.

Plate 87

Doorways.

Porch at Balbardie House, Bathgate

(*Designed by Robert Adam in West Lothian, Scotland*)

· ELEVATION ·

· SECTION ·

· PLAN ·

: BALBARDIE : HOUSE :
: BATHGATE :

Robt Adam 1792

Measured and Drawn by R. Philip Shaw.

Plate 89

Doorways.

Above : As the house was about sixty years ago. Below : As it is today.

Porch, at Wimborne, Dorset.

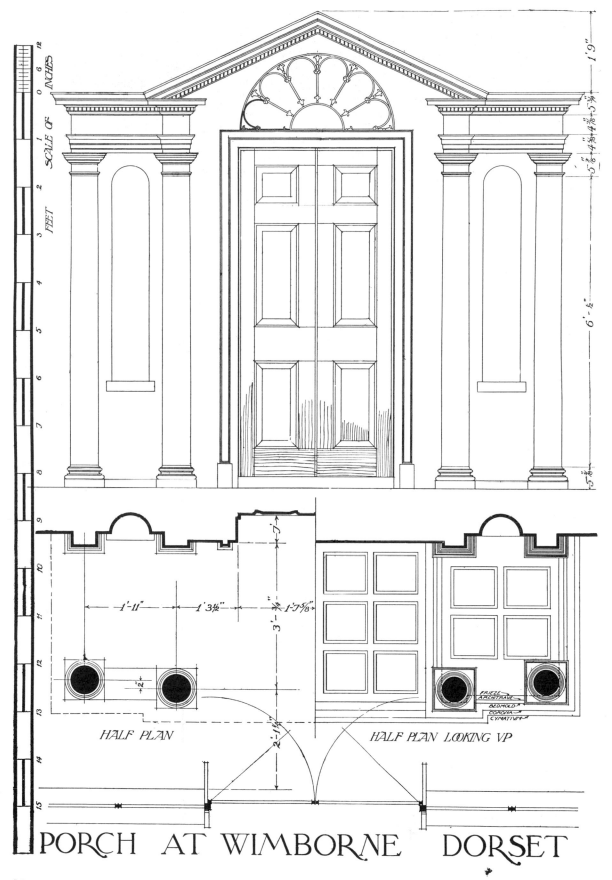

PORCH AT WIMBORNE DORSET

Measured and Drawn by H. A. McQueen and Ernst V. West.

Plate 91

Doorways.

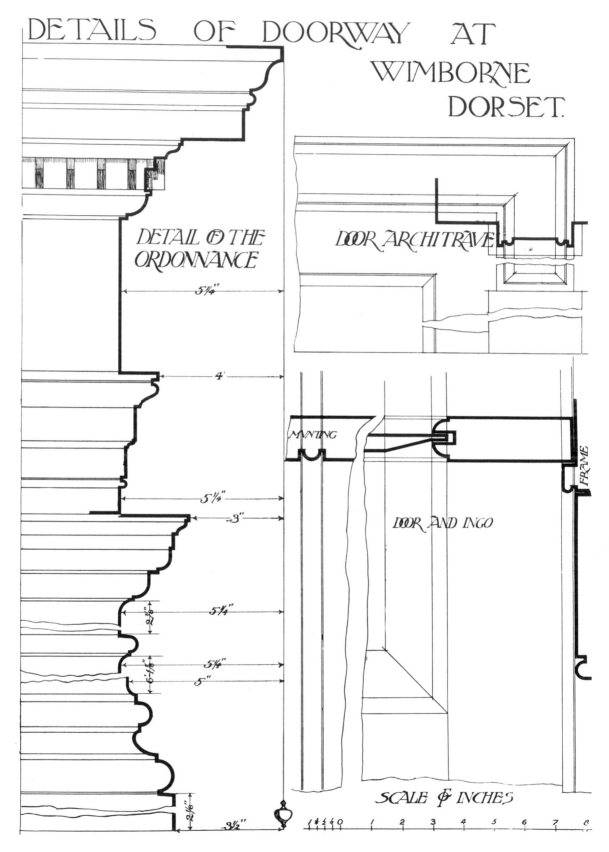

DETAILS OF DOORWAY AT WIMBORNE DORSET.

DETAIL OF THE ORDONNANCE

DOOR ARCHITRAVE

5¼"

4'

5¼"

3"

MVNTING

DOOR AND INGO

FRAME

5¼"

2⅜"

5¼"

6⅞"

5"

2⅖"

3½"

SCALE OF INCHES

1 ¾ ½ ¼ 0   1   2   3   4   5   6   7   8

Measured and Drawn by H. A. McQueen and Ernst V. West.

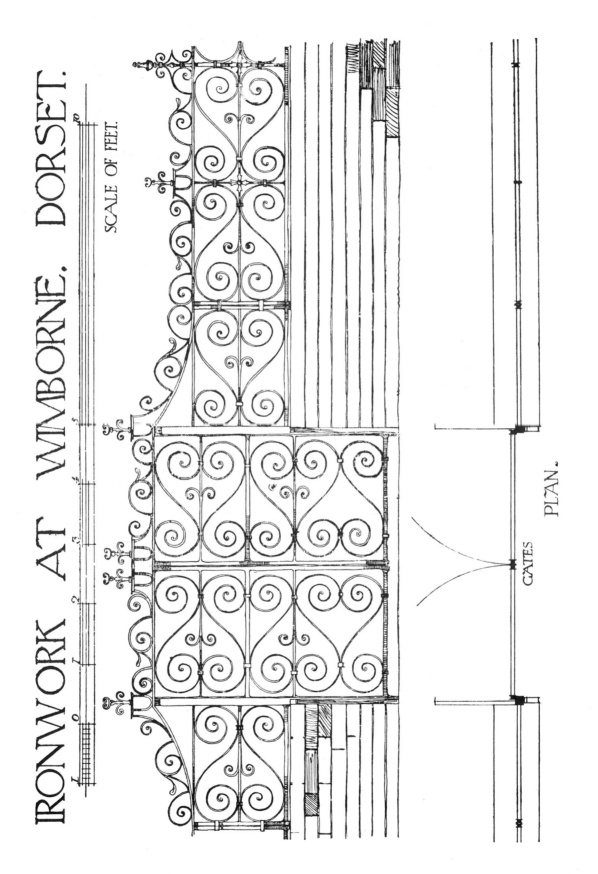

IRONWORK AT WIMBORNE. DORSET.

SCALE OF FEET.

GATES PLAN.

Measured and Drawn by H. A. McQueen and Ernst V. West.

Plate 93

Doorways.

Doorway, Wimborne, Dorset.

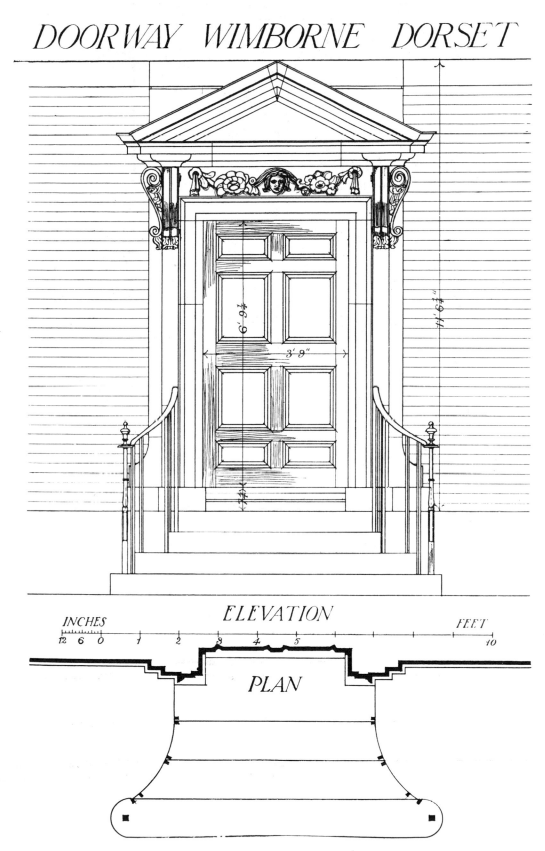

DOORWAY WIMBORNE DORSET

ELEVATION

INCHES   FEET

12 6 0   1   2   3   4   5   10

PLAN

Measured and Drawn by Theo. G. Scott.

Plate 95

Doorways.

DETAILS OF DOORWAY
WIMBORNE DORSET

DETAILS OF
IRONWORK

INCHES

FFFT

Measured and Drawn by Theo. G. Scott.

Gateways and Ironwork

Notes on Plates 96—107

Plates 96–97

Gateway in The Close, Salisbury, Wiltshire.
This gateway and the next one, both in the Close at Salisbury, are good examples of early Georgian ironwork. This one has good solid stone piers topped with carved pineapples, and, on each side of the gate, there are simple wrought-iron panels of scroll pattern. The gate itself is totally simple—just straight bars with some trifling cresting. The light and delicate lamp carrier over the gate is a very attractive feature.

Plates 98–99

No 68 The Close, Salisbury, Wiltshire.
Similar but on a larger scale to the previous one, this gateway has been given added importance by the railings on each side. The only elaboration is in the scroll panels; otherwise, straight bars and fine smithwork contribute to the eminently satisfying and simple design. A pair of brick and stone piers finished off by ball finials complete this pleasing example, which is presumably of the same date as the house standing behind, which was built about 1710.

Plates 100–101

Wrencote, Croydon, Surrey.
This fine gateway and railings once adorned the forecourt of Wrencote, Croydon, built about 1720 and an outstanding example of its period. In *Plate 100* the front doorway can be seen, with beast's heads carved on the brackets. The exterior details of this house are illustrated in *Plates 23–25*.

Plates 102–103

No 5 Cheyne Walk, Chelsea, London.
Nikolaus Pevsner has described these gates as 'sumptuous', and they certainly are. It has been suggested that they came from nearby Lindsay House and that they were made for Count Zinzendorf in about 1750. They do seem to be somewhat too large and magnificent for the house behind, but they have their own scale, emphasized by the tall brick piers with their carved stone urns.

Plates 104–105

Nos 11 and 12 Barnhill, Stamford, Lincolnshire.
Unlike the majority of London railings, where every upright bar is let into the stone, this example from Stamford has a kind of cillpiece raised above the stone by a few inches. Support is given by stouter bars being taken through the cill and mortised into the stonework at regular intervals. A feature of these railings is the alternately decorated heads of the individual bars. The work is late seventeenth century.

Plates 106–107

Railings: Bocking Church, Essex.
These are very attractive churchyard railings, and they are also interesting for their construction. The upright bars at the side of the panels pass through the horizontal piece at the top and, instead of being rivetted, they are fixed with a pin. The horizontal bars are finished off with some decoration, and a flat piece is provided on top of them to carry the crestings.

Plate 96   Gateways and Ironwork.

From the Close, Salisbury, Wilts.

DETAIL OF CORNICE
TO PIERS

From the Close, Salisbury, Wilts.

Measured and Drawn by J. M. W. Halley.

Plate 98 Gateways and Ironwork.

From the Close, Salisbury, Wilts.

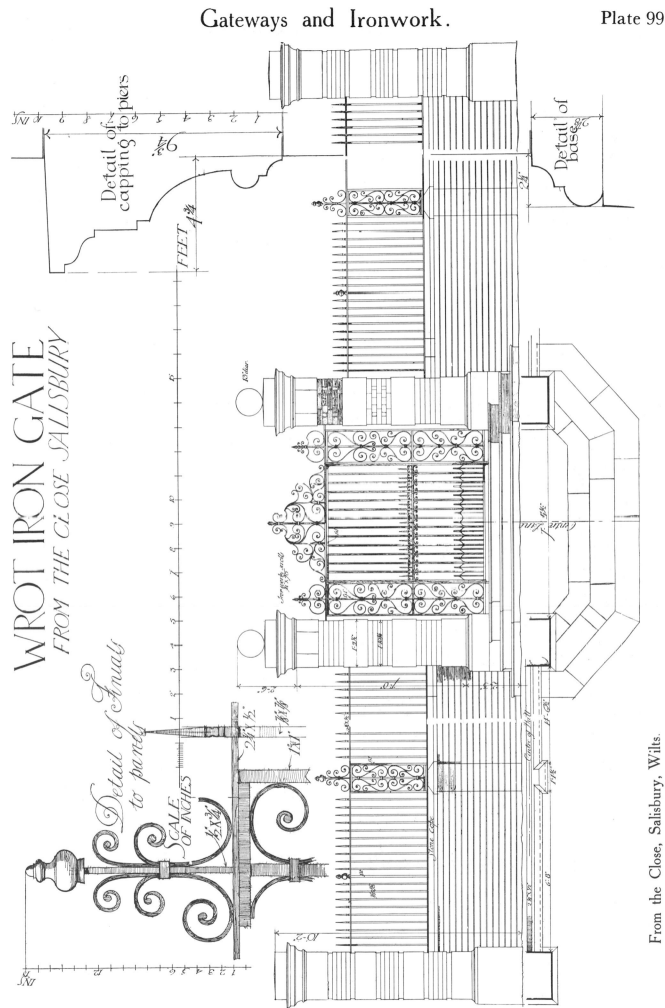

WROT IRON GATE
FROM THE CLOSE SALISBURY

Detail of capping to piers

Detail of base

Detail of Finials to panels

SCALE OF INCHES

From the Close, Salisbury, Wilts.

Measured and Drawn by J. M. W. Halley.

Plate 100   Gateways and Ironwork.

The Entrance Gate, Wrencote, Croydon, Surrey.

Scale of Feet

Ins 12 0 1 2 3 4 5 6 ft.

| WRENCOTE | CROYDON | ENTRANCE GATE | d1720 |

Measured and Drawn by Christopher J. Woodbridge.

Plate 102

Gateways and Ironwork.

The Gates, No. 5, Cheyne Walk, Chelsea, London.

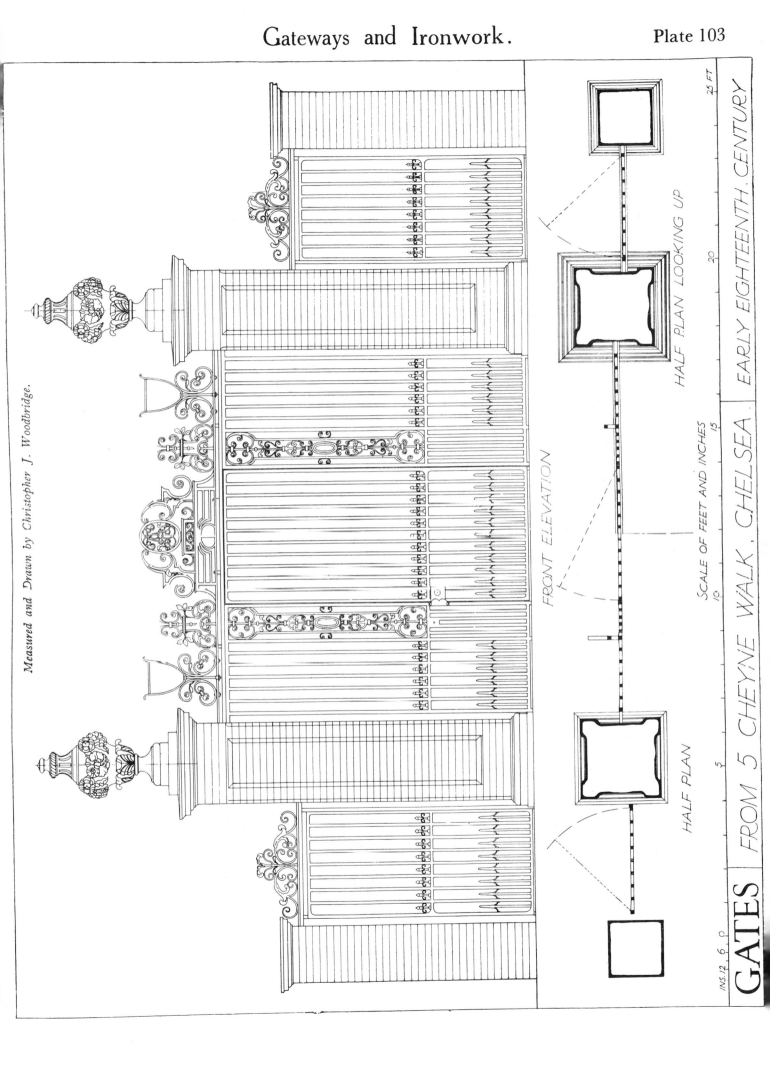

Measured and Drawn by Christopher J. Woodbridge.

FRONT ELEVATION

HALF PLAN LOOKING UP

HALF PLAN

SCALE OF FEET AND INCHES

INS.12 6 0   5   10   15   20   25 FT

GATES FROM 5 CHEYNE WALK, CHELSEA. EARLY EIGHTEENTH CENTURY.

Plate 104   Gateways and Ironwork.

Details of Wrought-iron Railings to No. 11, Barnhill, Stamford.

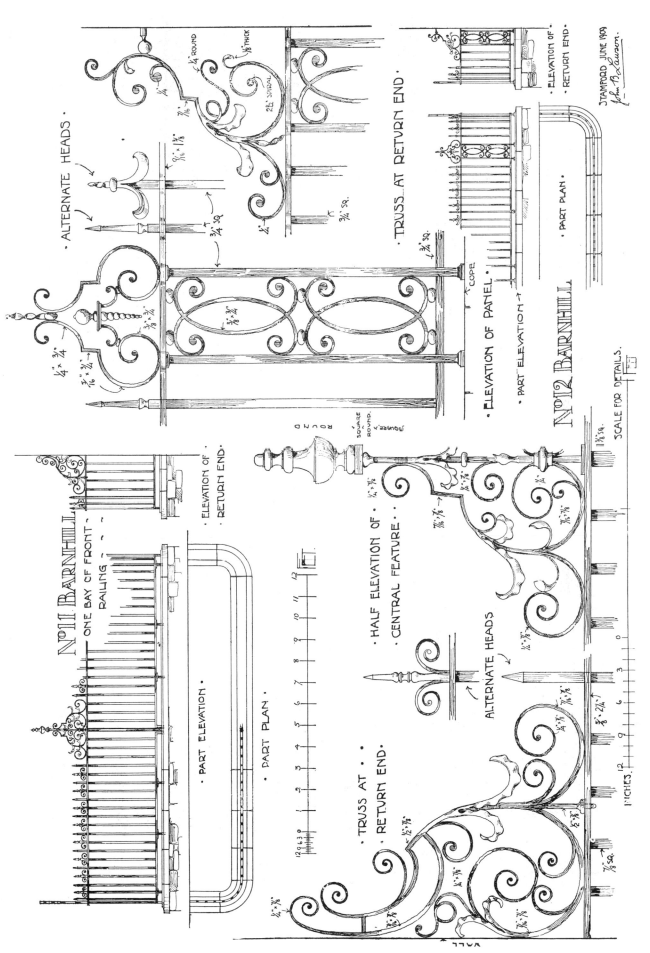

· ALTERNATE HEADS ·

· TRUSS AT RETURN END ·

· ELEVATION OF · RETURN END ·

STAMFORD JUNE 1909
John B. Lawson.

· ELEVATION OF PANEL ·

· PART ELEVATION →

· PART PLAN ·

· N⁰ 12 BARNHILL ·

ROUND.
SQUARE.
ROUND.

· HALF ELEVATION OF · CENTRAL FEATURE ·

ALTERNATE HEADS

SCALE FOR DETAILS.

INCHES.

· N⁰ 11 BARNHILL ·

ONE BAY OF FRONT · RAILING ·

· ELEVATION OF · RETURN END ·

· PART ELEVATION ·

· PART PLAN ·

· TRUSS AT · RETURN END ·

Measured and Drawn by John B. Lawson.

Plate 106

Gateways and Ironwork.

Wrought-iron Railings, Bocking Church, Essex.

WROT IRON RAILINGS

at Bocking Church Essex

Stay

Feet

Inches

Measured and Drawn by Theo. G. Scott.

Interiors

Notes on Plates 108—165

Plates 108–113

Sudbrook Park, Petersham, Surrey.

This villa was designed by James Gibbs about 1728 for John Campbell, Duke of Argyll. The chief feature of the interior is the Cube Room of thirty feet. This room is full of superb carving. Some reports suggest that Gibbs used J. M. Rysbrack to execute the sculpture and carvings. The chimney-piece bearing the Argyll arms surrounded by military trophies is exceptionally fine (see the *frontispiece*). Nathaniel Lloyd, in his book *The History of the English House*, says that 'everything was sacrificed to the Cube Room; indeed two staircases were needed to reach the first floor apartments, separated by the upper part of this room.'

The top illustration in *Plate 110* is taken from James Gibbs's *Book of Architecture*, published in 1728, and shows his original design for the front of the house. The drawing below, presumably by Gibbs himself, of the east wall of the Cube Room comes from the Gibbs' Collection in the Ashmolean Museum, Oxford. It should be compared with *Plates 111 and 112*. This house is now the club house of the Richmond Golf Club.

Plates 114–145

No 26 Hatton Garden, London.

The general arrangement of the rooms of this house, now sadly demolished, can be seen from the plan of the staircase and hall (*Plate 115*). The dining and breakfast rooms are on the ground floor (marked 'Committee Room' and 'Museum') and on the first floor are the two drawing rooms (marked 'Cambridge Ward' and 'Skinners Ward'). The reason why some of the rooms were called 'wards' was because, in the nineteenth century, the house belonged to a philanthropic doctor who converted it into a hospital for patients needing orthopaedic treatment. From this beginning sprang a famous institution, for eventually the hospital moved to Stanmore and is now known as the Royal National Orthopaedic Hospital.

The floor pattern in the staircase hall, laid in marble, is drawn in Batty Langley's *The City and Country Builder's and Workman's Treasury of Design*. The staircase is a very graceful one, with its low handrail and the long curved ramps joining it to the newels (*Plate 114*).

The interior of the house is an excellent example of a simple but well executed early eighteenth-century London home. The panelling in deal is of the ordinary type: a plain ovolo moulding with raised panels and a dividing chain rail. On the lower floors an architrave, frieze and cornice were used to finish the panelling but, on the second floor, a bold, plaster cornice was all that was used. The dining room (*Plates 116–125*) is a delightful room, which it is still possible to see since it is now preserved in the Victoria and Albert Museum, South Kensington. Almost every carving is vigorously carved, and the fronts of the cupboards are made of fine mahogany. The doors (*Plate 122*) are topped by a cartouche similar to the one in James Gibbs's book of 1732.

The fireplaces in the house vary in quality and style. In the dining room and breakfast room the carving is first rate but the proportions of the upper parts are unsatisfactory. The one in the drawing room (*Plate 126*) is of a much better design, with a large frame to take a picture.

A complete set of photographs and measured drawings of a house like this one is useful in giving some idea of the skill and patience that went into the creation of an early eighteenth-century London house. It was built at a time when, as Nathaniel Lloyd says, 'never has the workmanship of this period been excelled'.

Plates 146–157

Bourdon House, Berkeley Square, London.

Built in 1721–5, the house belongs to the early period of the development of the area around Berkeley Square by the Grosvenor family. The architect is unknown but the house has considerable charm, coming from the small and intimate nature of its early Georgian rooms. The ante-dining room has excellent panelling and a very fine chimney-piece. Angelica Kauffmann has been credited with the painting in the chimney-piece panels. The library door is very rare (*Plate 154*). It is curved on plan and contains a kind of transom in a circular-headed niche of sufficient dimensions to take a life-size bust.

In style, the door looks like the work of Adam. This house, once the London home of the Duke of Westminster, is now the premises of Mallett at Bourdon House Ltd.

Plates 158–161
Bradmore House, Hammersmith, London.
This is an early eighteenth-century house, attributed to Thomas Archer. Most of the internal fittings have now been destroyed, but the panelled room (*Plates 159, 160*) is preserved at the Geffrye Museum, Kingsland Road, London, E2. The house has not been demolished: it still stands in Queen Caroline Road, Hammersmith, looking neglected and having lost its roof balustrading and urns. It now serves as offices and a bus garage for London Transport—a far cry from the time when it was probably the most handsome house in the village of Hammersmith. *Plate 158* shows the exterior as it used to be.
The view, below, of a room in the central part of the house shows the quality of the panelling that used to exist. *Plates 159* and *160* are drawings of a smaller room in the north wing. A brick niche

from the garden has also been preserved by the Geffrye Museum.

Plates 162–163
Doorway, Gwydyr House, Whitehall, London.
This doorway is one of many others inside this house which, although heavily decorated, do in fact fit in well with the dignified way in which the building as a whole has been designed. The doorway has Corinthian pilasters, decorated architrave and a carved frieze at the head. It reflects the skill of the architect who built the house in 1772—at a reputed cost of £6000—for Sir Peter Burrell (Surveyor-General of Crown lands) who later became Lord Gwydyr.
Gwydyr House has had many successive owners, including the Reform Club in 1838. It is now the Welsh Office.

Plates 164–165
Fanlight at 35 Bedford Square, London.
This delicately designed fanlight surmounts one of the internal doors of the Architectural Association School of Architecture.

Carving over Niche on East Elevation

Brackets on E & W Doors

Carving over Doors, East & West Elevations.

Carving in the Cube Room, Sudbrook Park, (Drawn by Theo. G. Scott and B. R. Penderel Brodhurst).

Plate 108   Interiors.

Cube-Room, Sudbrook Park, Petersham, Surrey.

Built about 1728. Architect: James Gibbs. (See also the Frontispiece)

GOLF CLUB HOUSE
SUDBROOK PARK
PETERSHAM

Window Seat

Window Architrave

Skirting

Panel Moulding

THE CAPITAL

THE BASE

THE GREAT ENTABLATURE

Inches 0 2 4 6 8 10 12 14 16 18 20 22 24

Measured and Drawn by Theo. G. Scott and B. R. Penderel Brodhurst.

Plate 110   Interiors.

Sudbrook Park, Petersham, Surrey.

At top: James Gibbs' original design for the front elevation (from his Book
of Architecture). *Above: Gibbs' drawing for the east wall of the Cube
Room (see Plates 111 and 112). (By courtesy of the Ashmolean Museum, Oxford)*

East Side of Cube-Room, Sudbrook Park, Petersham, Surrey.

Plate 112

Interiors.

SUDBROOK GOLF HOUSE   PETERSHAM

Carving here

A rosette in

each coffer

Carving here

Carving here

East Elevation

Plan looking down

Scale of 0 6 12 Feet

Measured and Drawn by Theo. G. Scott and B. R. Penderel-Brodhurst.

SUDBROOK GOLF HOUSE PETERSHAM

Carving here

A rosette in each coffer

Carving here

Carving here

South Elevation

Plan through Pilasters looking up

Scale of 0   6   12 Feet

Measured and Drawn by Theo. G. Scott and B. R. Penderel-Brodhurst.

Plate 114   Interiors.

Staircase formerly at No. 26, Hatton Garden, City of London

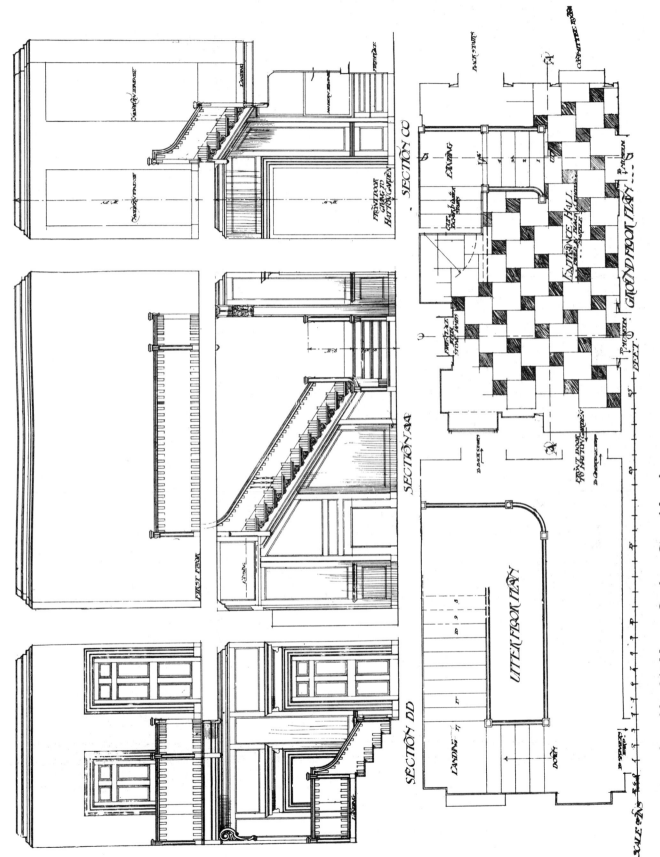

Staircase formerly at No. 26, Hatton Garden, City of London

Measured and Drawn by J. M. W. Halley.

Plate 116   Interiors.

Dining Room, formerly at No. 26, Hatton Garden   (*Now in the Victoria and Albert Museum, Kensington.*)

Alcove at side of Fireplace.

Dining Room, formerly at No. 26, Hatton Garden, City of London.

Plate 118

Interiors.

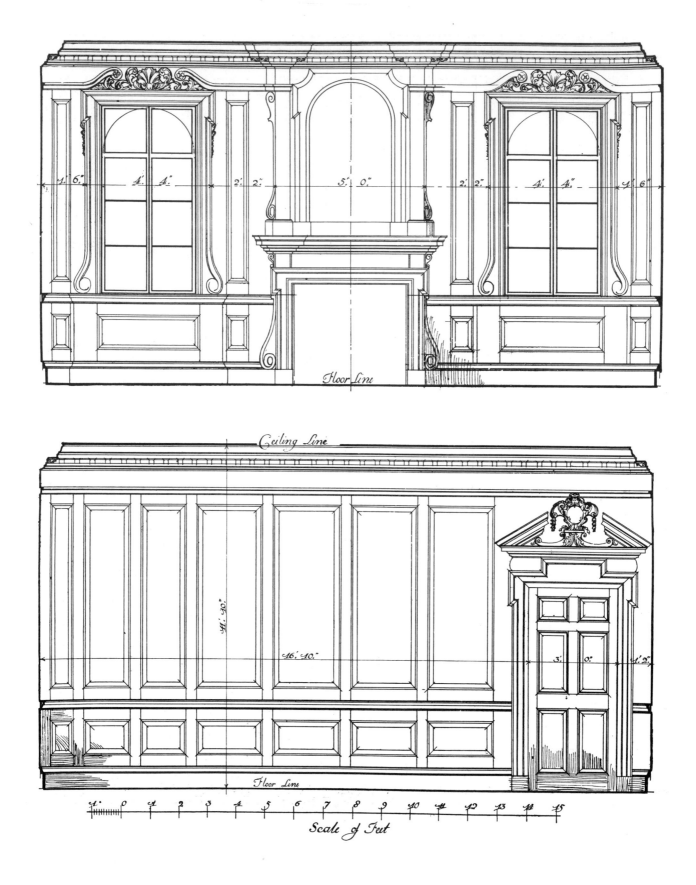

Dining Room, formerly at No. 26, Hatton Garden, City of London.
Measured and Drawn by J. M. W. Halley and H. A. McQueen.

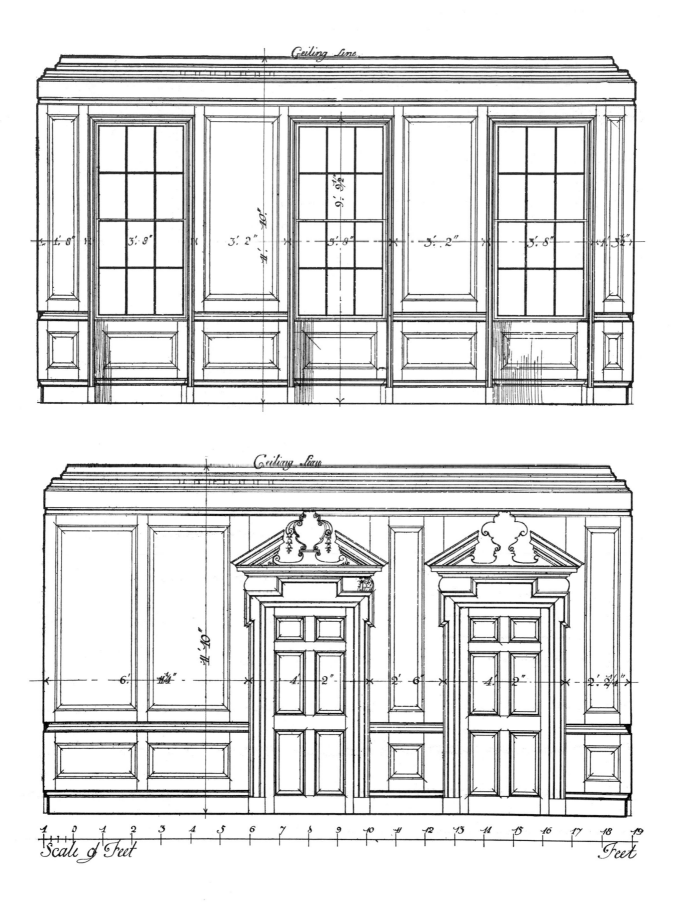

Dining Room, formerly at No. 26, Hatton Garden, City of London.

Measured and Drawn by J. M. W. Halley and H. A. McQueen.

Plate 120   Interiors.

Dining Room, formerly at No. 26, Hatton Garden, City of London.

Ceiling Line

Centre Line of Fireplace

Scale of Feet

5' 5"

3' 11"

7¼

5' 4¾"
3' 5½"
4' 0"

Floor Line

Measured and Drawn by J. M. W. Halley and H. A. McQueen.

Plate 122   Interiors.

Dining Room, formerly at No. 26, Hatton Garden, City of London.

DETAIL OF
DOORWAY

4' 2" over architrave

7' 0"

7" — 3½" — 12½" — 4" — 12½" — 3½" — 7"

Centre Line of Door

5½"

4' 2"

1½"

6' 4"

6½"

Measured and Drawn by J. M. W. Halley and H. A. McQueen.

Plate 124

Interiors.

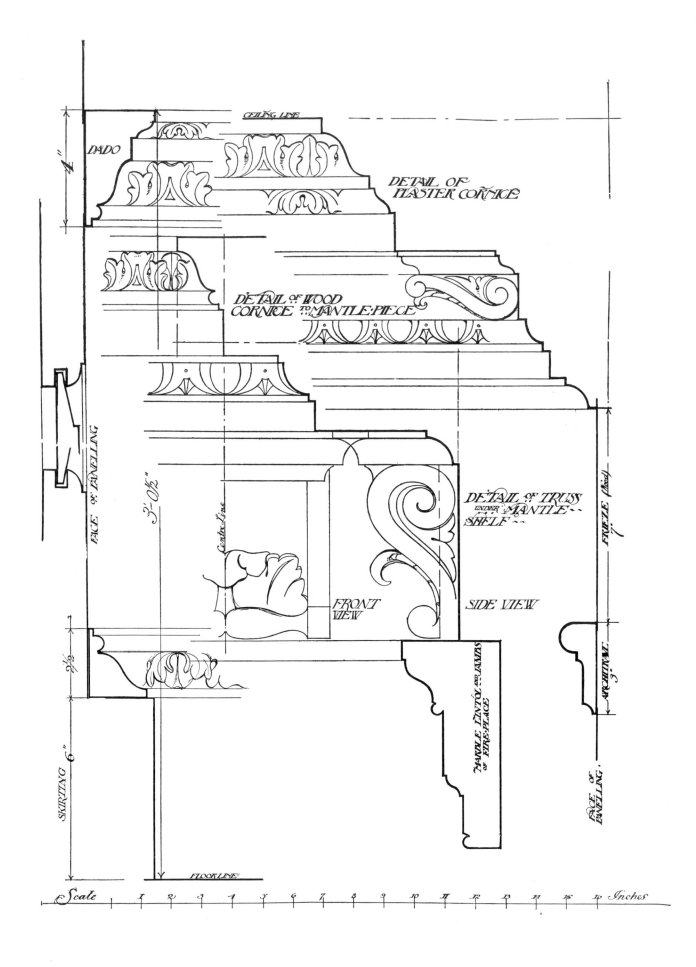

DADO

DETAIL OF PLASTER CORNICE

CEILING LINE

DETAIL OF WOOD CORNICE TO MANTLE·PIECE

FACE OF PANELLING

3'-0½"

Centre Line

DETAIL OF TRUSS UNDER MANTLE SHELF

FRONT VIEW

SIDE VIEW

FRIEZE (Plain) 7"

MANTLE LINTOL AND JAMBS OF FIRE·PLACE

ARCHITRAVE 3"

FACE OF PANELLING.

2½"

SKIRTING 6"

FLOOR LINE

Scale   1   2   3   4   5   6   7   8   9   10   11   12   13   14   15   16   Inches

Details Dining Room, formerly at No. 26, Hatton Garden, City of London,
Measured and Drawn by J. M. W. Halley and H. A. McQueen.

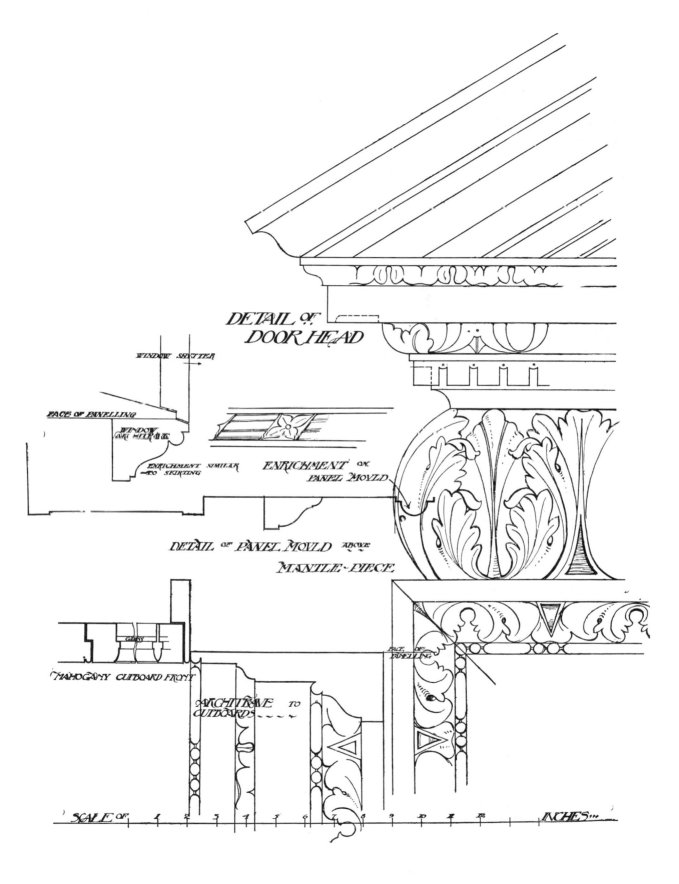

DETAIL OF
DOOR HEAD

WINDOW SHUTTER

FACE OF PANELLING

WINDOW
ARCHITRAVE

ENRICHMENT SIMILAR
TO SKIRTING

ENRICHMENT ON
PANEL MOULD

DETAIL OF PANEL MOULD ABOVE

MANTLE-PIECE

GLASS

MAHOGANY CUPBOARD FRONT

FACE OF
PANELLING

ARCHITRAVE TO
CUPBOARDS

SCALE OF 1 2 3 4 5 6 7 8 9 10 11 12 INCHES

Dining Room, formerly at No. 26, Hatton Garden, City of London.

Measured and Drawn by J. M. W. Halley and H. A. McQueen.

Plate 126

Interiors.

Mantelpiece in Drawing Room, formerly at No. 26, Hatton Garden

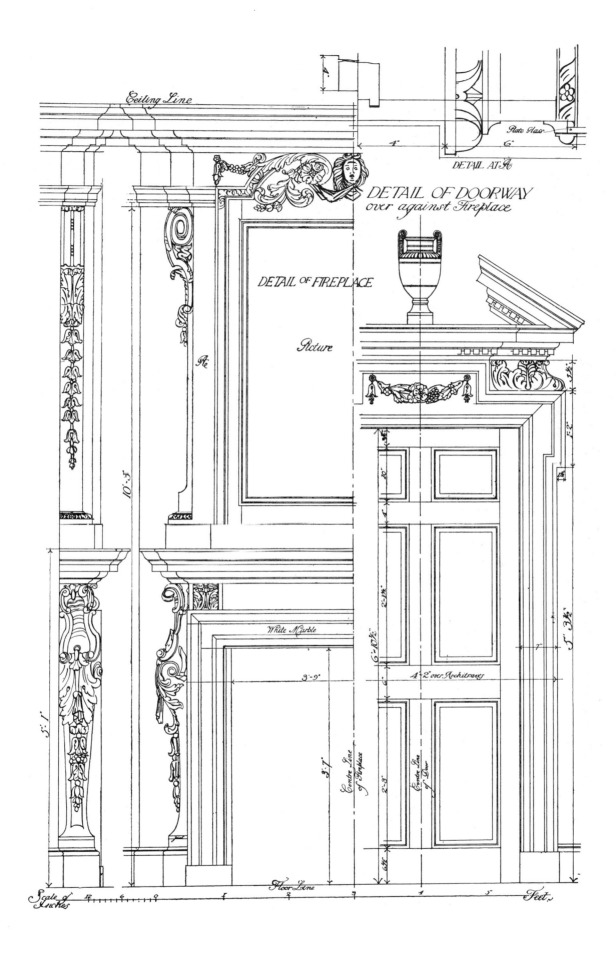

Ceiling Line

DETAIL AT A

DETAIL OF DOORWAY
over against Fireplace

DETAIL OF FIREPLACE

Picture

White Marble

4'·2' over Architraves

Centre Line of Fireplace

Centre Line of Door

Floor Line

Scale of Inches

Feet

Measured and Drawn by J. M. W. Halley.

Plate 128   Interiors.

Drawing Room Door, opposite fireplace, formerly at No. 26, Hatton Garden

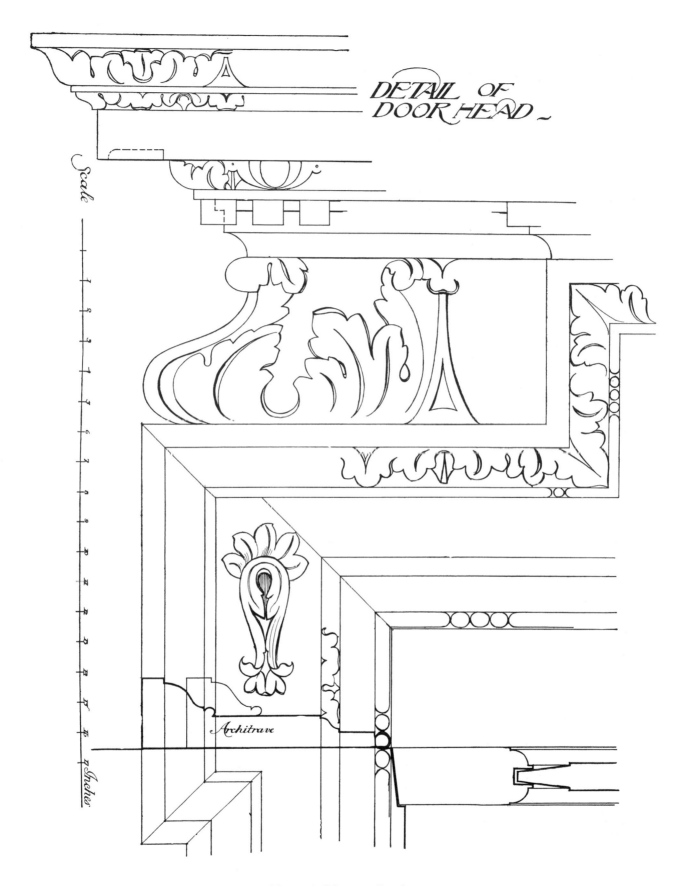

DETAIL OF
DOOR HEAD ~

Scale

Inches

Architrave

Drawing Room, formerly at No. 26, Hatton Garden
Measured and Drawn by J. M. W. Halley.

Plate 130   Interiors.

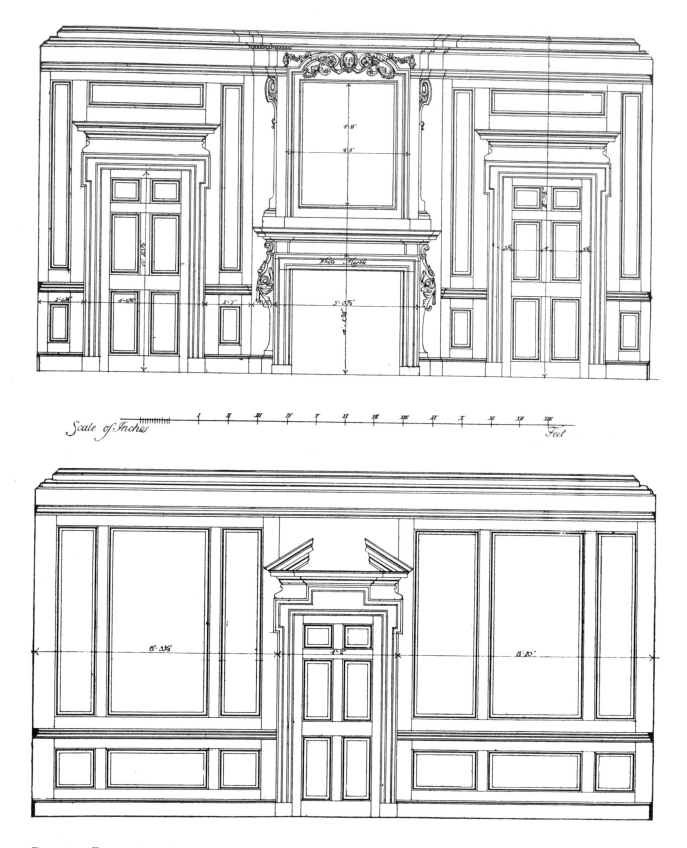

Scale of Inches   Feet

Drawing Room, formerly at No. 26, Hatton Garden, City of London.

Measured and Drawn by J. M. W. Halley.

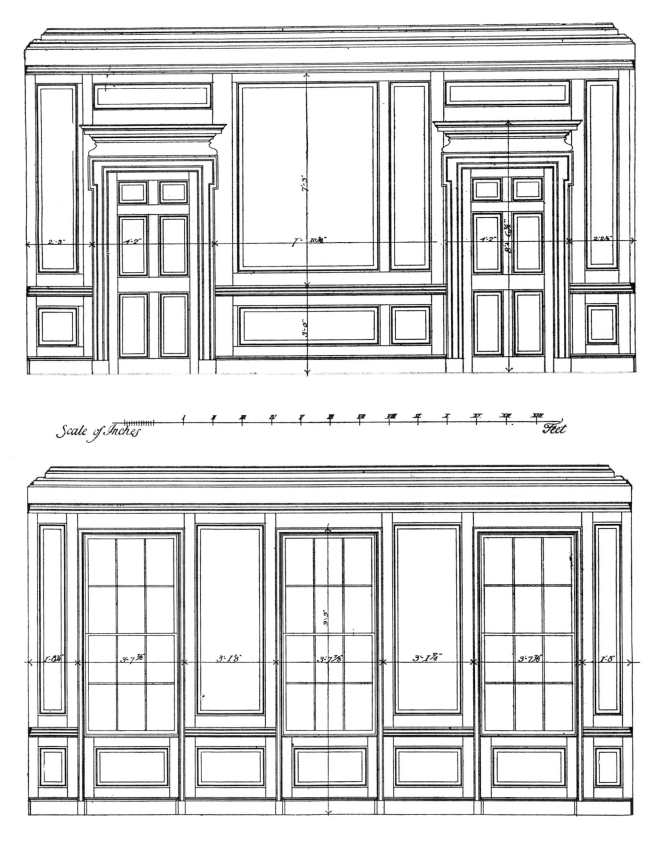

Scale of Inches

Feet

Drawing Room, formerly at No. 26, Hatton Garden, City of London.
Measured and Drawn by J. M. W. Halley.

Plate 132

Interiors.

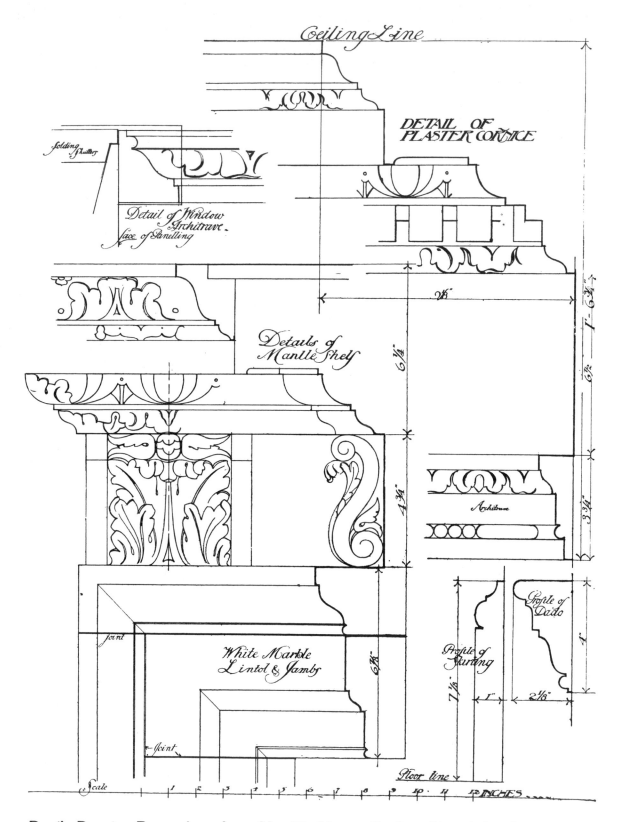

Ceiling Line

DETAIL OF
PLASTER CORNICE

Detail of Window
Architrave.
face of Panelling

folding Shutters

Details of
Mantle Shelf

Architrave

White Marble
Lintol & Jambs

Joint

Joint

Profile of
Dado

Profile of
Starting

Floor line

Scale ... INCHES ...

Details Drawing Room, formerly at No. 26, Hatton Garden, City of London.
Measured and Drawn by J. M. W. Halley.

Drawing Room, formerly at No. 26, Hatton Garden, City of London.

Plate 134   Interiors.

Doorway in "Skinner's Ward." No. 26, Hatton Garden

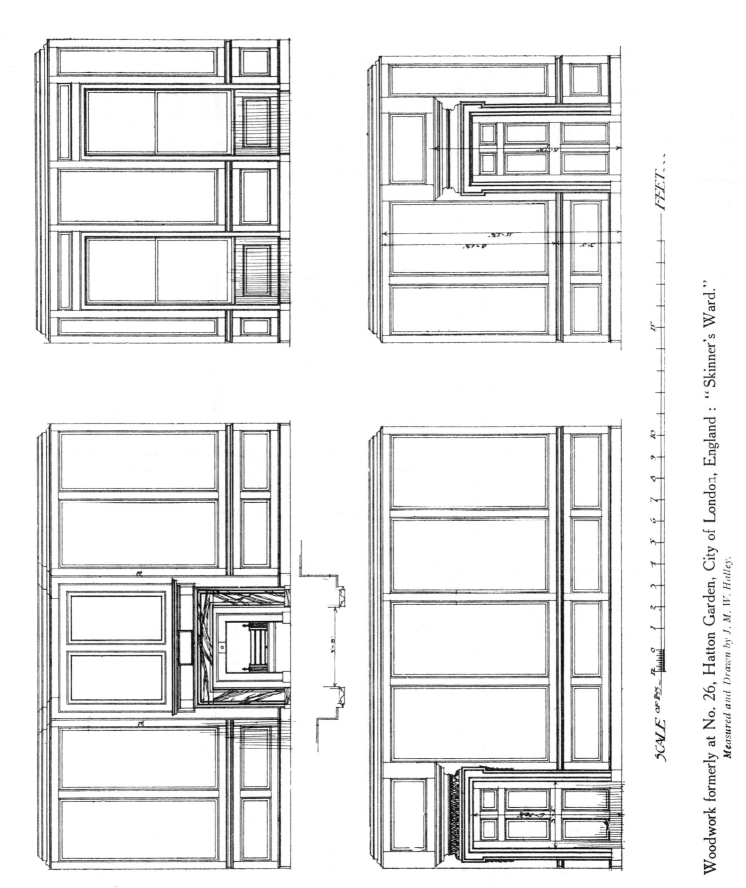

SCALE OF FEET

FEET

Woodwork formerly at No. 26, Hatton Garden, City of London, England : "Skinner's Ward."

Measured and Drawn by J. M. W. Halley.

Plate 136　　　　　　　Interiors.

Chimney-Piece in "Skinner's Ward."

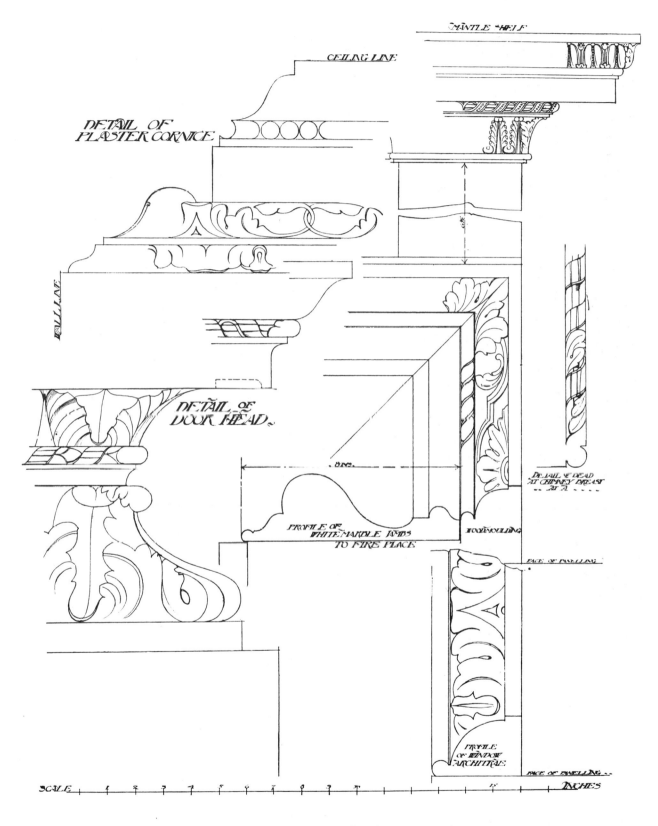

CEILING LINE

MANTLE SHELF

DETAIL OF
PLASTER CORNICE

WALL LINE

DETAIL OF
DOOR HEAD.

ONE.

PROFILE OF
WHITE MARBLE JAMBS
TO FIRE PLACE

DETAIL OF BEAD
AT CHIMNEY BREAST
AT A

BODY MOULDING

FACE OF PANELLING

PROFILE
OF WINDOW
ARCHITRAVE

FACE OF PANELLING

SCALE   INCHES

Details of " Skinner's Ward."   No. 26, Hatton Garden, City of London

Measured and Drawn by J. M. W. Halley.

Plate 138   Interiors.

Breakfast Room, formerly at No. 26, Hatton Garden, City of London.

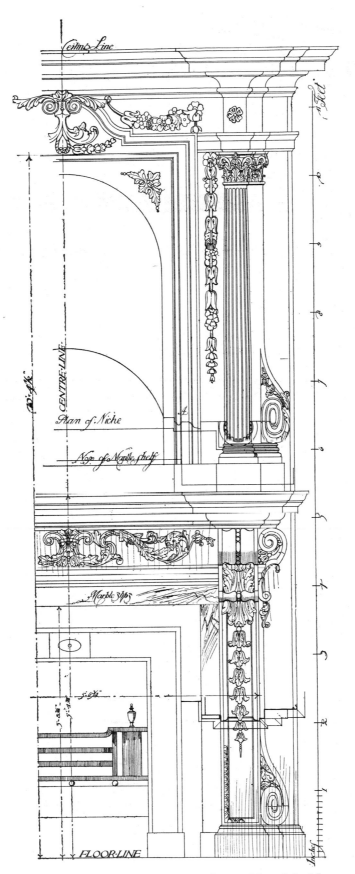

Details of Fireplace, Breakfast Room, formerly at No. 26, Hatton Garden

Measured and Drawn by J. M. W. Halley.

Plate 140

Interiors.

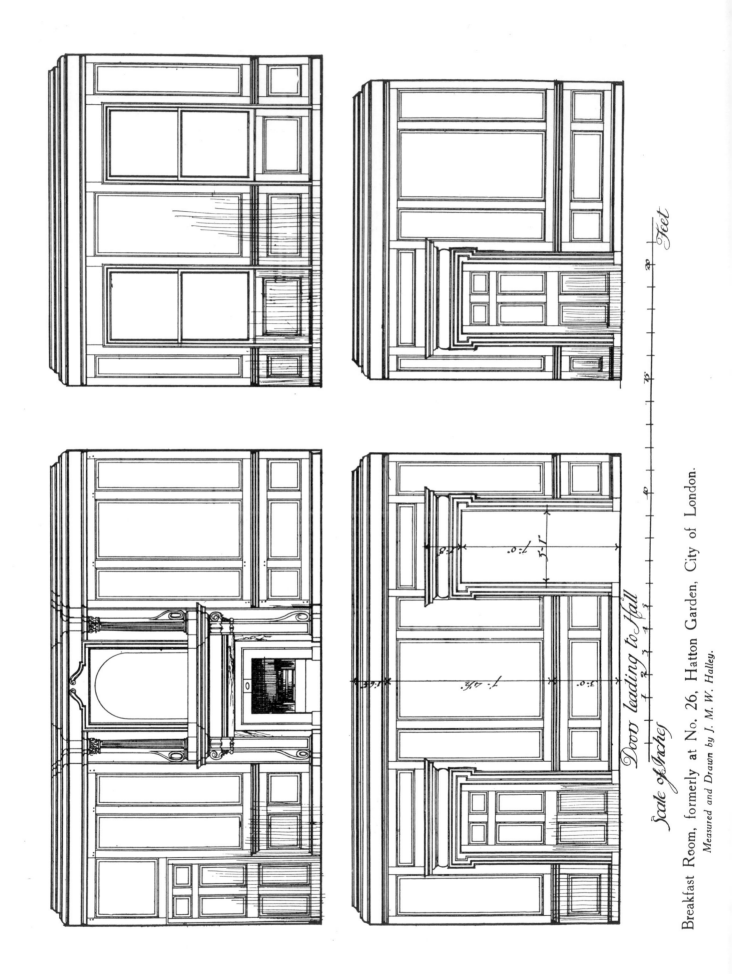

Scale of Inches

Door leading to Hall

Breakfast Room, formerly at No. 26, Hatton Garden, City of London.

Measured and Drawn by J. M. W. Halley.

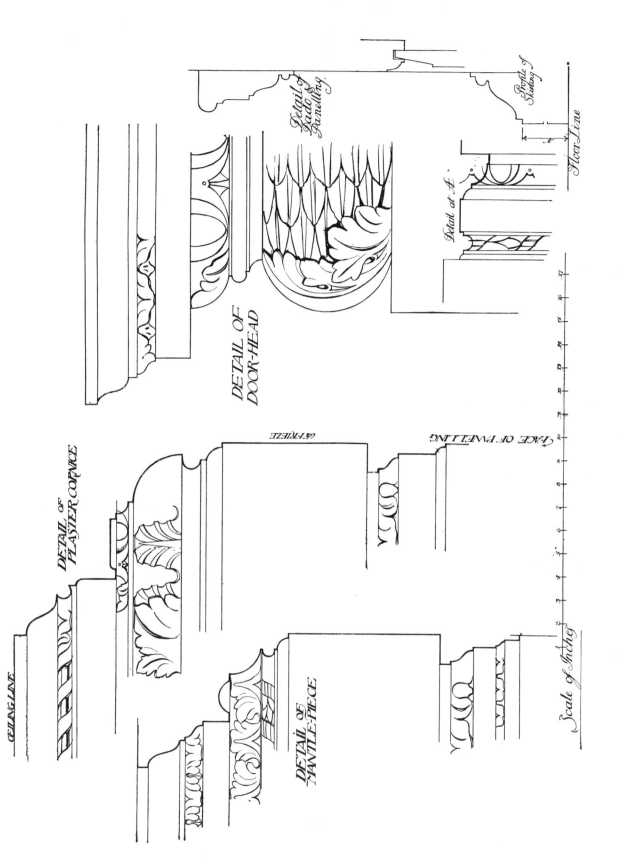

DETAIL OF
DOOR-HEAD

DETAIL OF
PLASTER CORNICE

DETAIL OF
MANTLE-PIECE

CEILING LINE

FRIEZE

FACE OF PANELLING

Detail of
Dado &
Panelling.

Detail at A.

Profile of
Skirting

Floor Line

Scale of Inches

Details Breakfast Room, formerly at No. 26, Hatton Garden,
City of London.

Measured and Drawn by J. M. W. Halley.

Plate 142   Interiors.

Breakfast Room, formerly at No. 26, Hatton Garden, City of London.

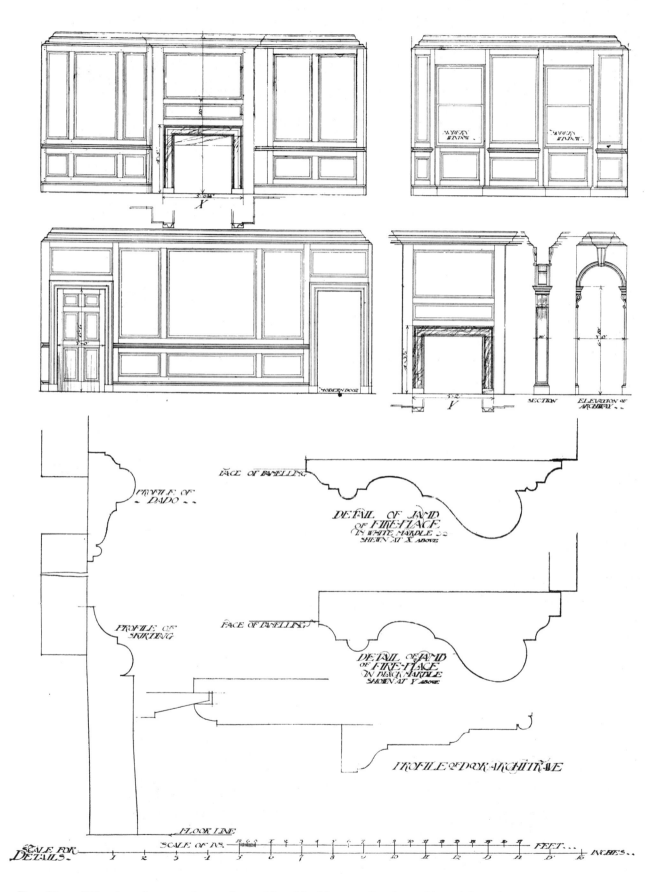

Panelling, Woodwork, etc., formerly at No. 26, Hatton Garden, City of London
Details of Archway and Room on Second Floor.

Measured and Drawn by J. M. W. Halley.

Plate 144   Interiors.

Archway on Second-floor Landing.

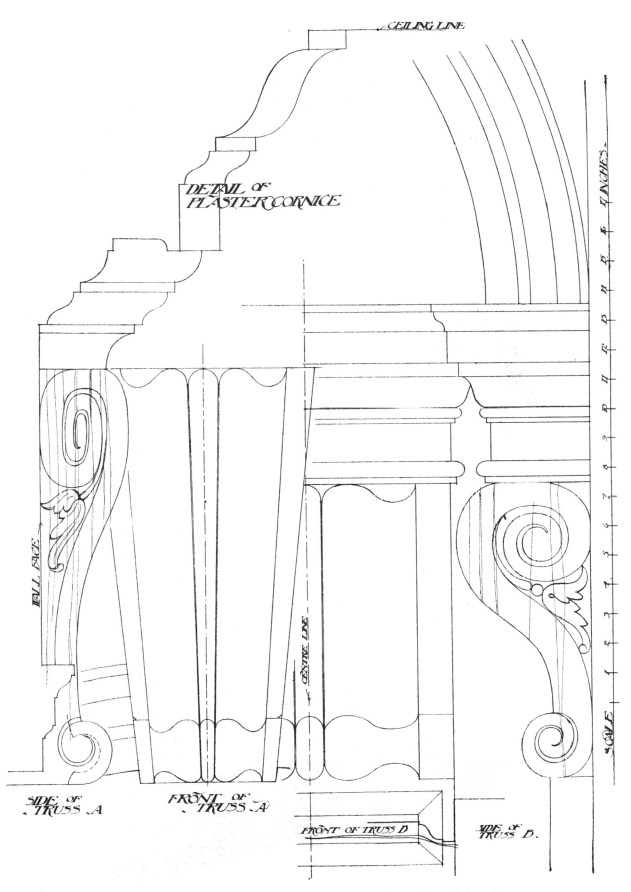

CEILING LINE

DETAIL OF
PLASTER CORNICE

WALL FACE

CENTRE LINE

SCALE

INCHES

SIDE OF
TRUSS A

FRONT OF
TRUSS A

FRONT OF TRUSS B

SIDE OF
TRUSS B

Panelling, Woodwork, etc., formerly at No. 26, Hatton Garden, City of London
Details of Archway on Second Floor.

Measured and Drawn by J. M. W. Halley.

Plate 146

Interiors.

Ante-Dining-room, Bourdon House, Bourdon Street, London.

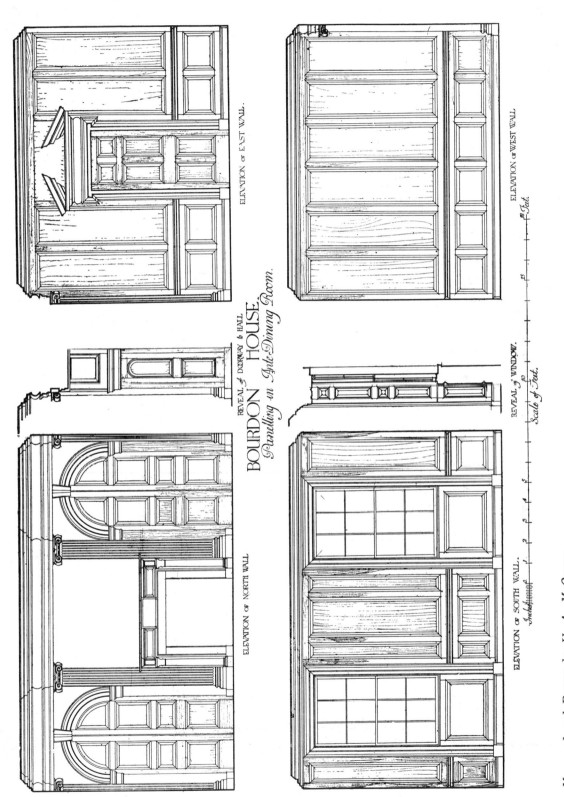

ELEVATION OF EAST WALL.

ELEVATION OF WEST WALL

ELEVATION OF NORTH WALL

ELEVATION OF SOUTH WALL.

REVEAL OF DOORWAY TO HALL

REVEAL OF WINDOW.

BOURDON HOUSE.
Panelling in Ante-Dining Room.

Scale of Feet.

Measured and Drawn by H. A. McQueen.

Plate 148   **Interiors.**

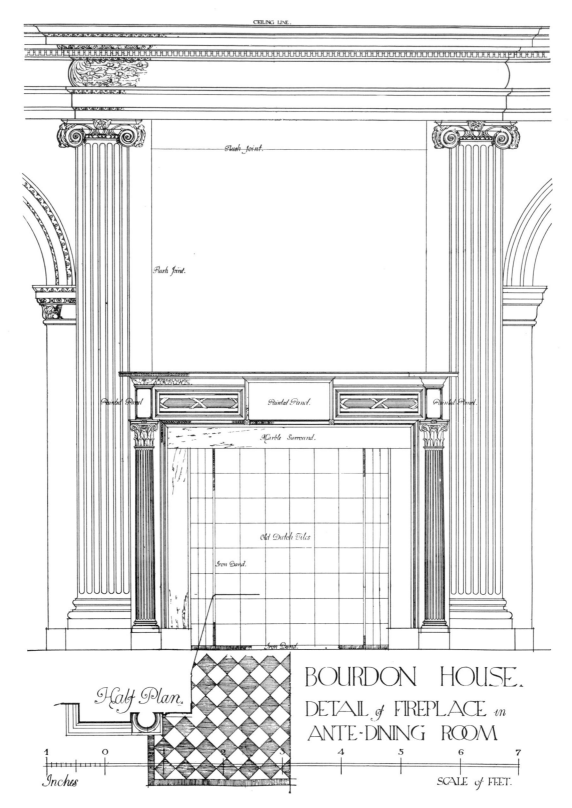

CEILING LINE.

Flush Joint.

Flush Joint.

Painted Panel.   Painted Panel.   Painted Panel.

Marble Surround.

Old Dutch Tiles.

Iron Band.

Iron Band.

Half Plan.

BOURDON HOUSE.
DETAIL of FIREPLACE in
ANTE-DINING ROOM

1   0   1   2   3   4   5   6   7

Inches   SCALE of FEET.

Measured and Drawn by H. A. McQueen.

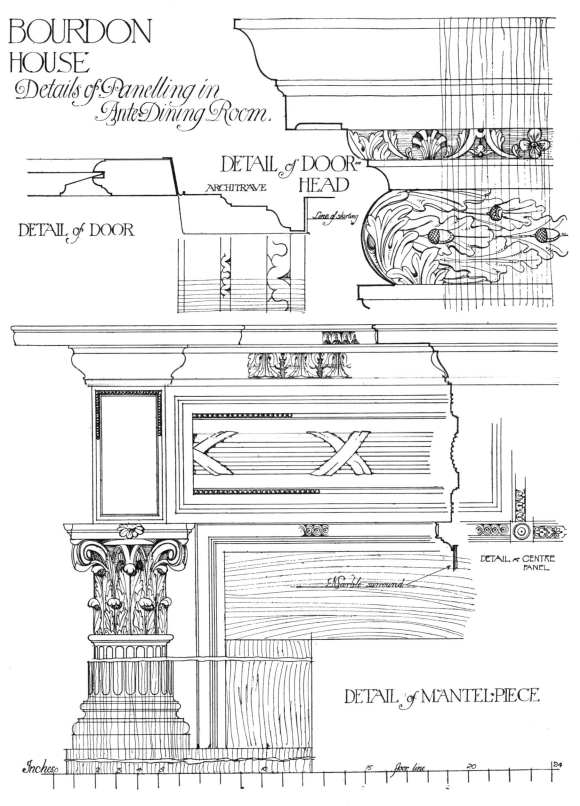

BOURDON
HOUSE.
*Details of Panelling in
Ante-Dining Room.*

DETAIL of DOOR-HEAD

ARCHITRAVE

DETAIL of DOOR

Line of skirting

DETAIL of CENTRE PANEL

Marble surround

DETAIL of MANTEL-PIECE

Inches

Measured and Drawn by H. A. McQueen.

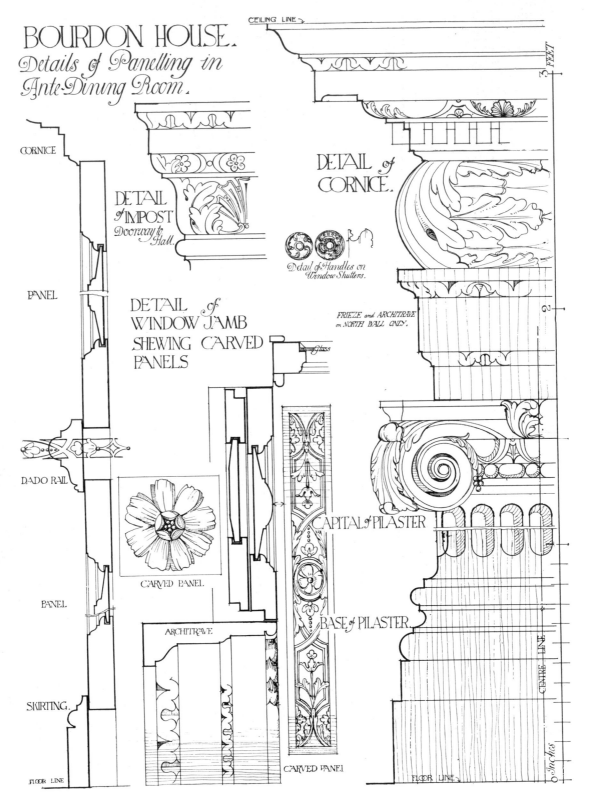

BOURDON HOUSE.
Details of Panelling in
Ante-Dining Room.

CEILING LINE

DETAIL of CORNICE.

CORNICE

DETAIL of IMPOST
Doorway to Hall.

DETAIL of WINDOW JAMB
SHEWING CARVED PANELS

PANEL

Detail of Handles on
Window Shutters.

FRIEZE and ARCHITRAVE
on NORTH WALL ONLY.

Glass

DADO RAIL

CAPITAL of PILASTER

CARVED PANEL.

PANEL

ARCHITRAVE

BASE of PILASTER.

SKIRTING.

CARVED PANEL

FLOOR LINE

CENTRE LINE

FLOOR LINE

3 FEET

O Inches

Measured and Drawn by H. A. McQueen.

Doorway in Ante-Dining-room, Bourdon House, Bourdon Street, London

Plate 152

Interiors.

Doorway in Ante-Dining-room, Bourdon House, Bourdon Street, London, W.

BOURDON HOUSE.

DETAIL of DOORWAY in ANTE-DINING ROOM

Measured and Drawn by H. A. McQueen.

Library Door, Bourdon House, Berkeley Square, London

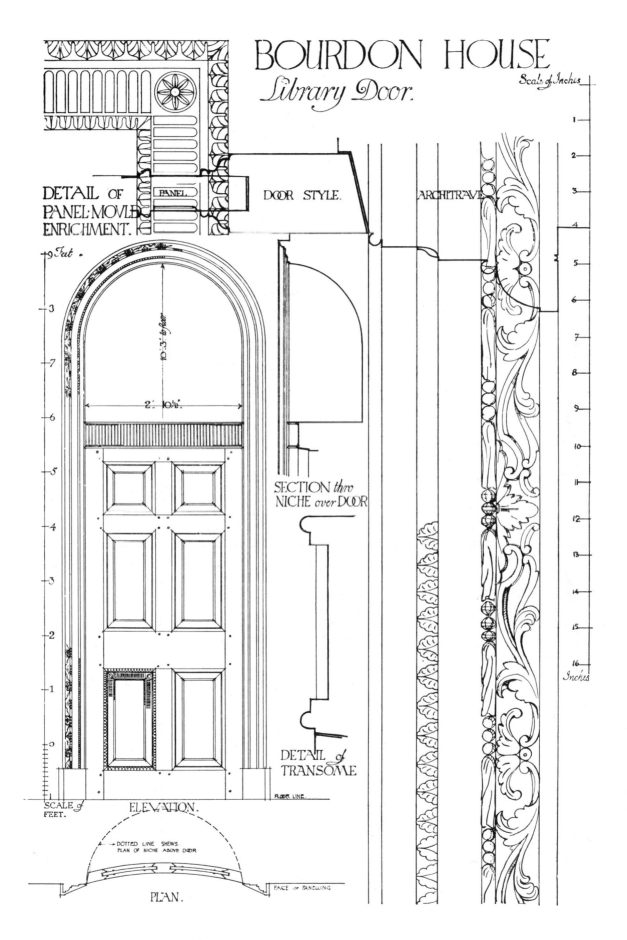

BOURDON HOUSE
Library Door.

Scale of Inches

DETAIL OF
PANEL·MOVLD·
ENRICHMENT.

PANEL

DOOR STYLE.

ARCHITRAVE.

SECTION thro
NICHE over DOOR

DETAIL of
TRANSOME

SCALE of
FEET.

ELEVATION.

FLOOR LINE.

DOTTED LINE SHEWS
PLAN OF NICHE ABOVE DOOR

FACE of PANELLING

PLAN.

Measured and Drawn by H. A. McQueen.

Plate 156　　　　　　　　Interiors.

Bedroom Fireplace, Bourdon House, Berkeley Square, London

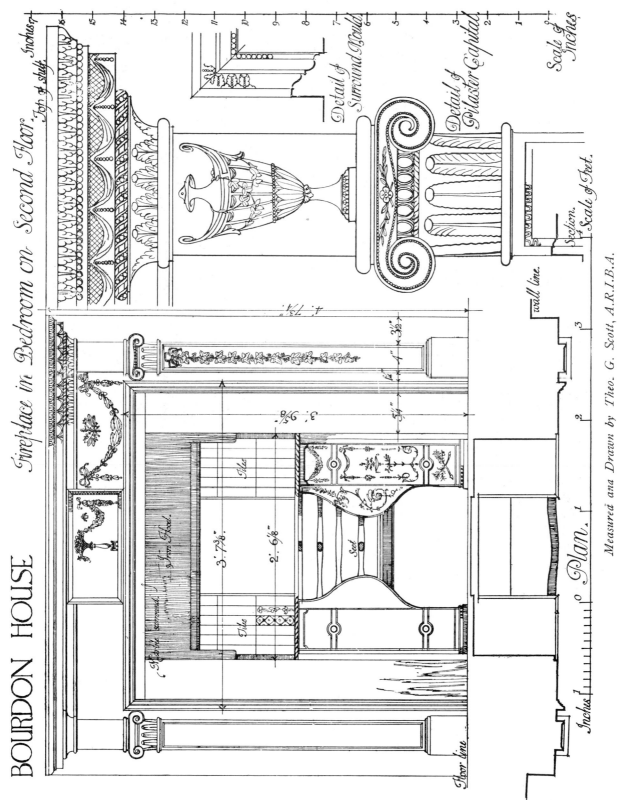

BOURDON HOUSE

Fireplace in Bedroom on Second Floor.

Top of shaft.

Detail of Surround Mould.

Detail of Plaster Capital.

Scale of Inches.

Scale of Feet.

Section.

wall line.

4′. 7¾″.

3′. 9⅝″.

3½″ *4″* *5½″*

Tiles.

Marble surround. 1 from floor.

3′. 7⅞″.

2′. 6⅛″.

Seat.

Tiles.

floor line.

Inches.

Plan.

Measured and Drawn by Theo. G. Scott, A.R.I.B.A.

Plate 158   Interiors.

*At top: the east front of Bradmore House, as it used to be. Above: a central first-floor
room, more ornately panelled than the north room shown in Plates 159, 160.*

Panelling from Bradmore House, Hammersmith, now in the Geffrye Museum, London.

Measured and Drawn by C. J. Woodbridge.

Plate 160

Interiors.

Plate 160

Panelling from Bradmore House, Hammersmith

Measured and Drawn by C. J. Woodbridge.

CEILING

BRADMORE HOUSE. HAMMERSMITH
DETAIL OF CARVED DEAL CORNICE TO NORTH
PANELLED ROOM ON FIRST FLOOR.

Reproduced by permission of the Greater London Council

Measured and Drawn by W. D. Quirke, A.R.I.B.A.

Plate 162

Interiors.

A Door and Doorcase at Gwydyr House, Whitehall, London.

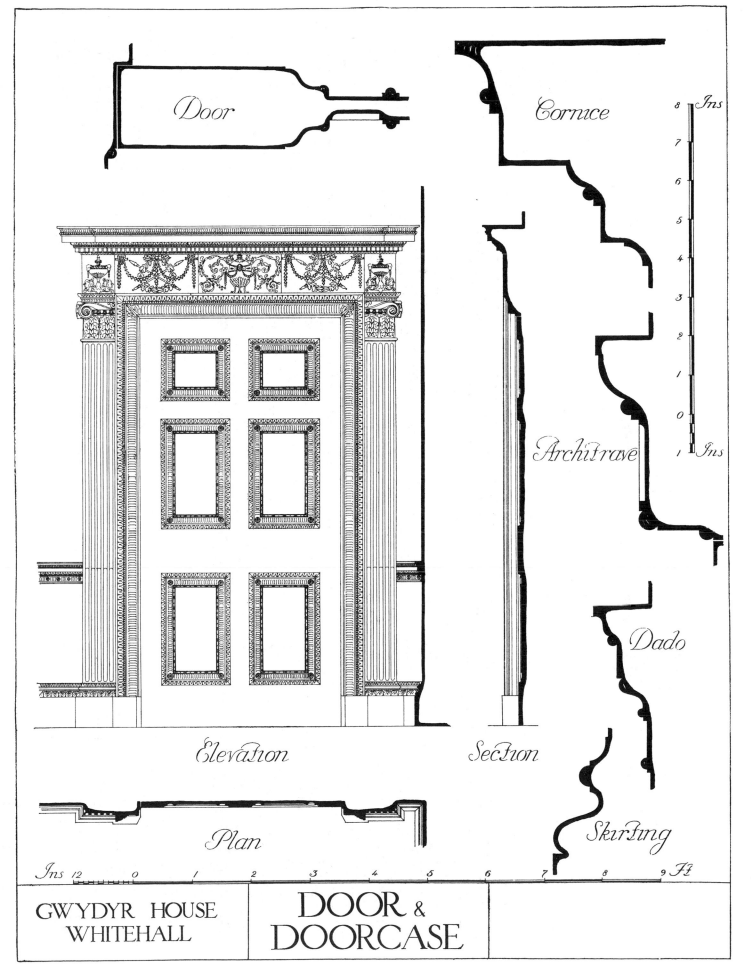

Door

Cornice

Architrave

Elevation

Section

Dado

Plan

Skirting

Measured and Drawn by Christopher J. Woodbridge.

Plate 164

Interiors.

A Fanlight from 35, Bedford Square, London.

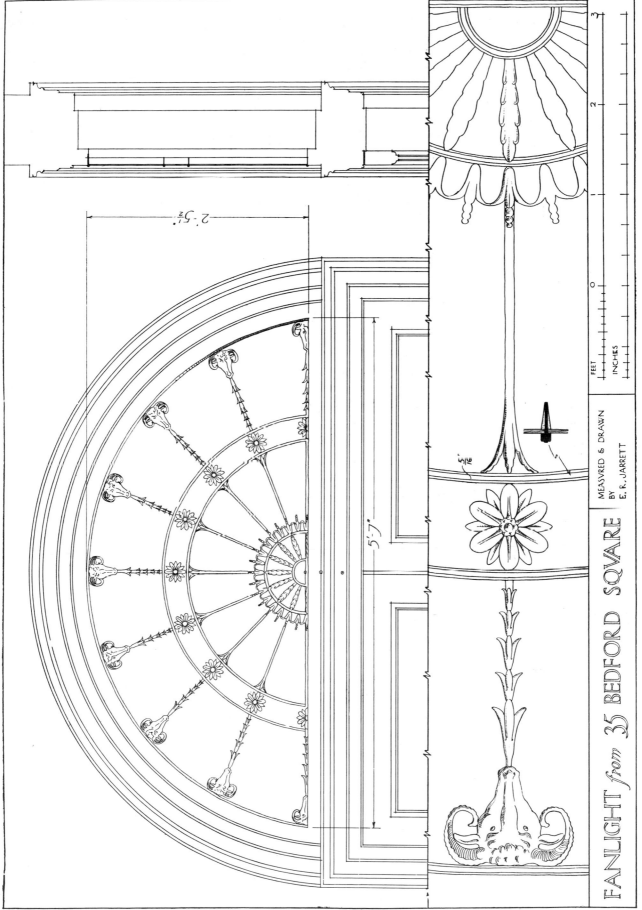

2'-5½"

5'-7"

$\frac{5'}{16}$

MEASVRED & DRAWN
BY
E. R. JARRETT

FEET

INCHES

FANLIGHT *from* 35 BEDFORD SQVARE

Measured and Drawn by E. R. Jarrett.

Chimney-pieces

Notes on Plates 166—191

Plates 166–171

Formerly in Coleman Street, London.

There must be few other Jacobean chimney-pieces that survived the Great Fire of London. One of the only parts of the city the fire never reached was the north end of Coleman Street, where this chimney-piece stood in the cedar-panelled room of an old house. However, what the Great Fire failed to do in 1666, a demolition squad succeeded in doing in 1896, although, luckily, the chimney-piece again escaped destruction It still remains as an exuberant and fanciful example of what *The Practical Exemplar* called 'the curious obsession of the Early Renaissance for monstrous and grotesque shapes'.

In a previous era, such elaborate work would have been done in marble or stone. Heavily carved wood chimney-pieces only appeared, to any extent, late in Elizabeth's reign when there was an upsurge in the joiner's craft.

Plates 172–175

The Metropolitan Water Board's Offices, Roseberry Avenue, London.

This chimney-piece was formerly in the seventeenth-century building of the New River Company, which was one of several ancient water-supply companies taken over by the Metropolitan Water Board. The entire room in which it stood (since called 'the Oak Room'), with its fine plasterwork, was transferred from the old building to the new offices of the Metropolitan Water Board in 1920. A. B. Pilling, Clerk of the Board, described the mantelpiece in a booklet published by the Water Board many years ago. 'The mantelpiece' he wrote, 'is of solid oak upon which is imposed a beautifully carved representation of the arms of William III. Much of the carving in the Oak Room—one of the delights of connoisseurs and certainly unique of its kind—is the work of Grinling Gibbons. . . The carving in places has reference to water affairs and the angler's gentle art, since it includes creels, water birds, all kinds of fishes, crayfish, water plants, as well as ears of corn, grasses, flowers and fruits. There is a festoon border to the Royal Arms thus carved of various things of this kind, which never fails to strike the visitor with its beauty.'

Plates 176–180

Old Rolls Office Mantelpieces (now in the Public Records Office, Chancery Lane, London).

Colen Campbell designed the old Rolls Office between 1717 and 1725. It was demolished in 1895. Campbell was the author of *Vitruvius Britannicus* and the architect of Burlington House, Piccadilly, Mereworth Castle, Kent, and Houghton Hall, Norfolk. These mantelpieces are now in the Public Records Office. The description in *The Architectural Review*, in 1920, of the one shown in *Plate 176* is still very apt. It said: 'The little mantelpiece illustrated here, now torn from its environment and bereft of its marble slips, is a piteous memorial of departed greatness. Gone is the polished grate which it enshrined, vanished like the brilliant society once grouped about its genial fireside; what remains, however, bears mute witness to the carver's skill, who wrought the fine ramps and rosettes from rude timber with well directed and incisive chisel.'

Plates 181–183

The Registrar-General's Office, Somerset House, London.

This handsome chimney-piece by Sir William Chambers is constructed of carved painted wood, enclosing slips of reddish hued veined marble. Chambers' own drawing shows the careful balance of this design. The novel Ionic pilaster capitals were his own invention.

Plates 184–185

The Library, Somerset House, London.

One of a pair in the library made of statuary marble which has now toned to the colour of old ivory. The carving of the lion-masks and the pendant husk drops is firm and dignified. When describing this chimney-piece and comparing Chambers with Robert and James Adam, *The Architectural Review* said 'his use of ornament was more sparing, his sense of scale more masculine.'

Plates 186–187

10 Henrietta Street, Dublin.

L. A. Shuffrey* divides eighteenth-century chimney-pieces into four broad types: those with

---

* *The English Fireplace* (Batsford).

plain or elaborate architrave only; with trussed pilasters; with caryatid or terminal figures; with column supports to the mantelshelf. This fine example is of the trussed pilaster type. It is by an unknown designer who, perhaps, gained inspiration from a pattern book. The cornice and frieze are richly decorated, and the trusses extend up to the cornice instead of being placed under the frieze—the more normal position. Thus greater length is given to the pilasters. The lining to the fireplace is of marble to protect the wood mantelpiece against fire. This chimney-piece would have been still better had the original firegrate not been replaced by a Victorian one.

Plates 188–189
Fireplace at 26 Hatton, Garden, London.
This late eighteenth-century fireplace was installed in one of the early eighteenth-century rooms of 26 Hatton Garden (now demolished). The interior of this house is illustrated in *Plates 114–145*. The slender, gracefully designed twin columns supporting the mantelshelf and the elegant decoration suggest the influence of Robert Adam.

Plates 190–191
Sir John Soane's Museum, Lincoln's Inn Fields, London.
Typical of Soane's work, this early nineteenth-century chimney-piece embodies a mirror which gives a curious feeling of spatial disturbance to the design. Soane had his own ideas about the importance of chimney-pieces: he liked the design to be fairly unobtrusive and treated as a base for a large mirror or other object above (in this case a picture) rather than as an important composition on its own.

Plate 166

Chimney-pieces

Early Renaissance Chimney-piece taken from a House in Coleman Street, London: E.C.

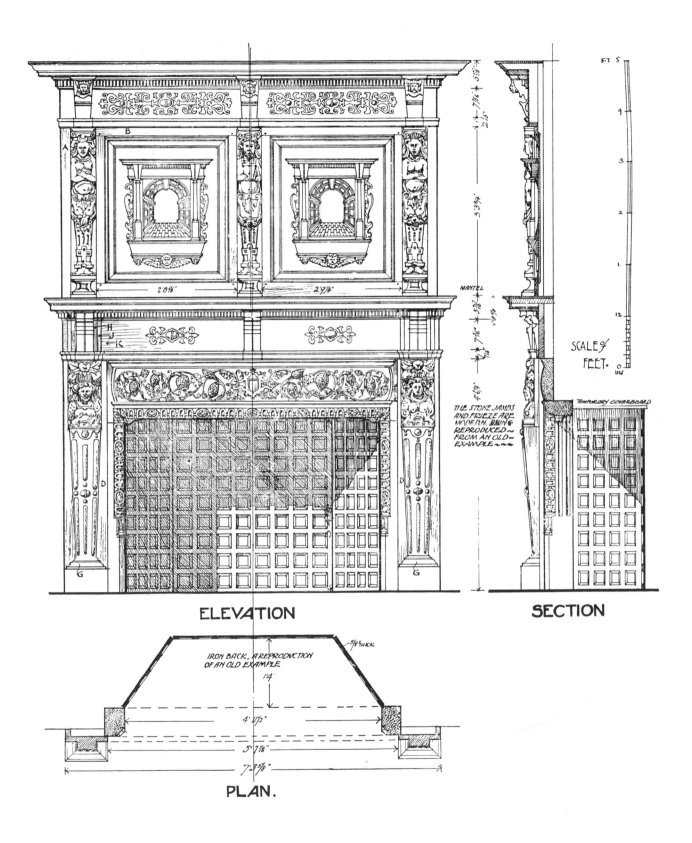

ELEVATION

SECTION

SCALE OF FEET.

THE STONE JAMBS AND FRIEZE ARE MODERN, BEING REPRODUCED FROM AN OLD EXAMPLE

TEMPORARY COVERBOARD

IRON BACK, A REPRODUCTION OF AN OLD EXAMPLE

PLAN.

Early Renaissance Chimney-piece taken from a House in Coleman Street, London, E.C.

Measured and Drawn by T. Frank Green, F.R.I.B.A.

Plate 168

Chimney-pieces

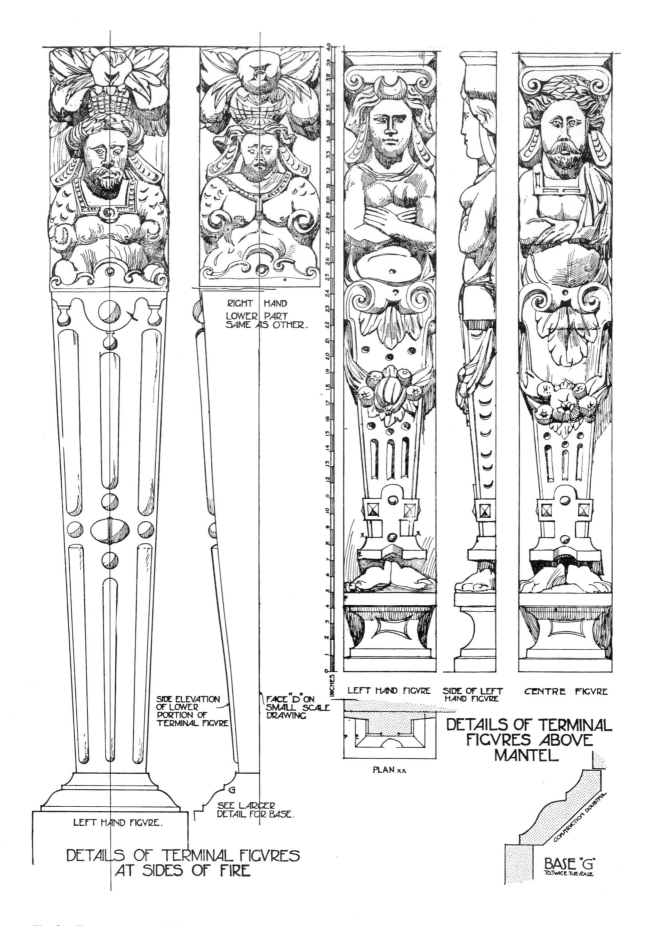

SIDE ELEVATION
OF LOWER
PORTION OF
TERMINAL FIGVRE

FACE "D" ON
SMALL SCALE
DRAWING

RIGHT HAND
LOWER PART
SAME AS OTHER.

G

SEE LARGER
DETAIL FOR BASE.

LEFT HAND FIGVRE.

DETAILS OF TERMINAL FIGVRES
AT SIDES OF FIRE

LEFT HAND FIGVRE   SIDE OF LEFT
HAND FIGVRE

CENTRE FIGVRE

PLAN xx

DETAILS OF TERMINAL
FIGVRES ABOVE
MANTEL

CONSTRVCTION DOVBTFVL

BASE "G"
TO TWICE THE SCALE

Early Renaissance Chimney-piece taken from a House in Coleman Street, London, E.C.

Measured and Drawn by T. Frank Green, F.R.I.B.A.

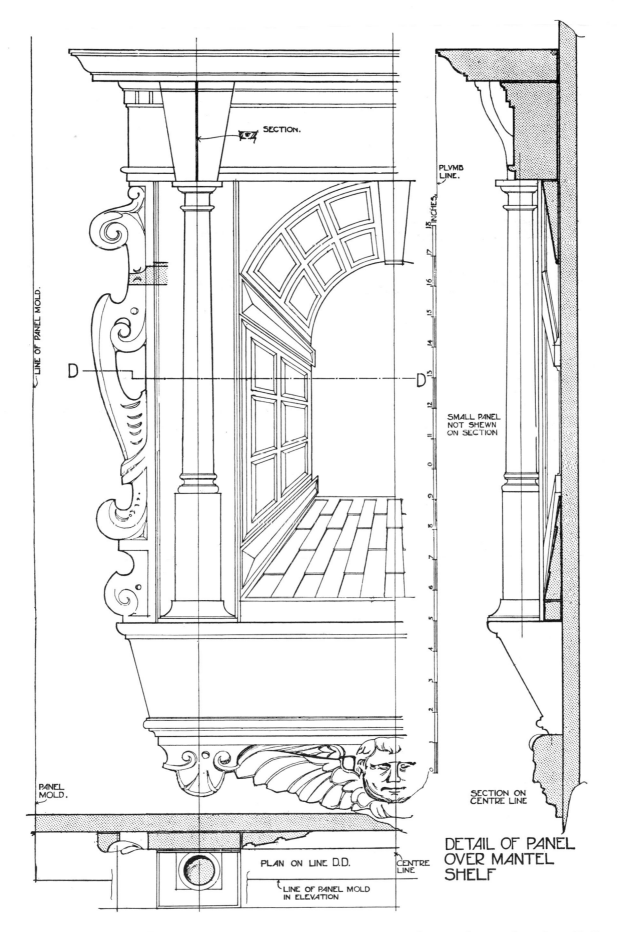

SECTION.

LINE OF PANEL MOLD.

D — D

PLVMB LINE.

SMALL PANEL
NOT SHEWN
ON SECTION

INCHES.

PANEL
MOLD.

SECTION ON
CENTRE LINE

PLAN ON LINE D.D.

CENTRE
LINE

LINE OF PANEL MOLD
IN ELEVATION

DETAIL OF PANEL
OVER MANTEL
SHELF

Early Renaissance Chimney-piece taken from a House in Coleman Street, London, E.C.

Measured and Drawn by T. Frank Green, F.R.I.B.A.

Plate 170   Chimney-pieces

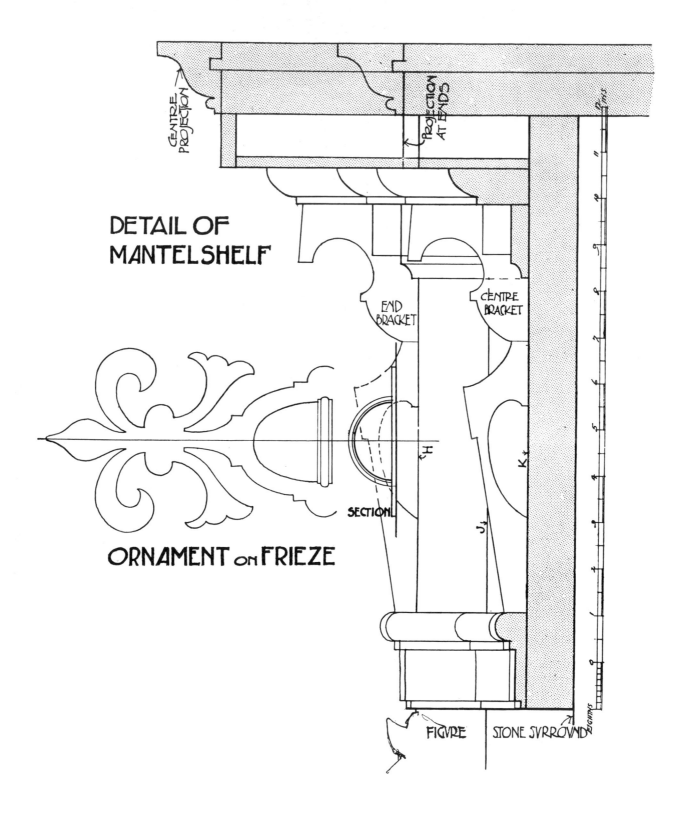

DETAIL OF
MANTELSHELF

ORNAMENT on FRIEZE

Early Renaissance Chimney-piece taken from a House in Coleman Street, London, E.C.

Measured and Drawn by T. Frank Green, F.R.I.B.A.

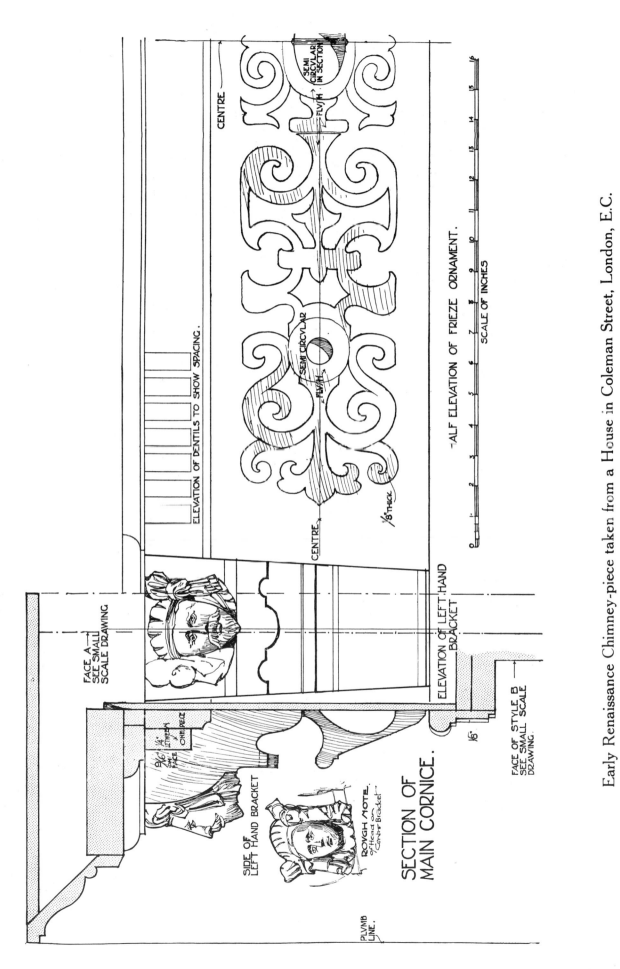

Early Renaissance Chimney-piece taken from a House in Coleman Street, London, E.C.

Measured and Drawn by T. Frank Green, F.R.I.B.A.

Plate 172   Chimney-pieces

The Metropolitan Water Board's "New River" Offices, Rosebery Avenue, Clerkenwell

Chimney-piece in the Oak Room

PLAIN PIECE TO MAKE OUT

MARBLE
WHITE, WITH DARK GREY VEIN

MARBLE
DARK GREEN BLACK
AND WHITE VEINS

IRON

MARBLE HEARTH

SCALE OF FEET

Measured and Drawn by T. Frank Green.

Plate 174   Chimney-pieces

Metropolitan Water Board's " New River " Offices, Rosebery Avenue, Clerkenwell, London

At top : the Oak Room. Above : detail of carving over chimney-piece.

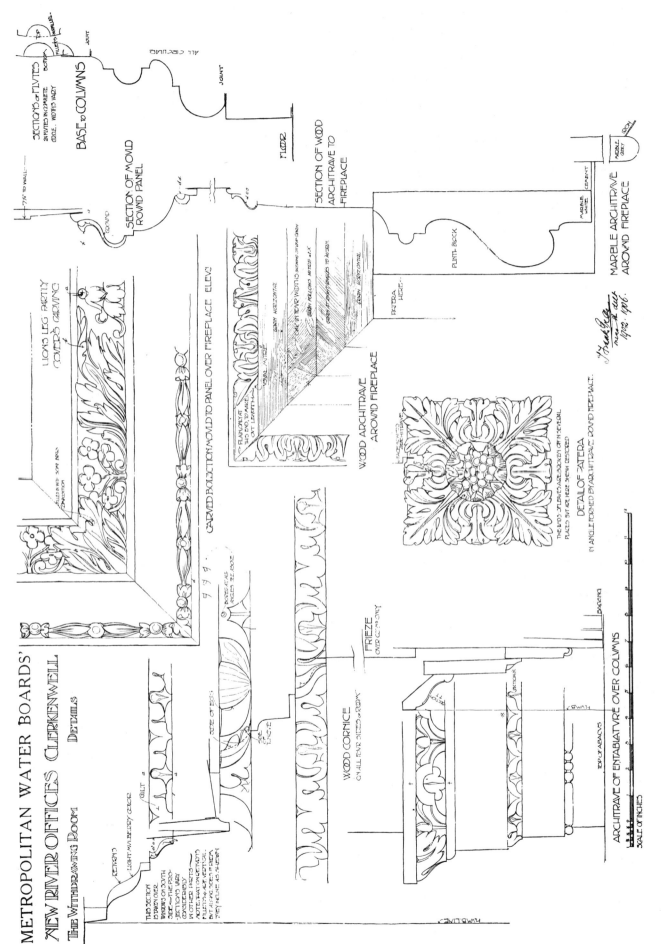

Measured and Drawn by T. Frank Green.

Plate 176   Chimney-pieces

Carved Wood Chimneypiece, from the Old Rolls Office, Chancery Lane, London.

From the
OLD ROLLS OFFICE
Chancery Lane

CHIMNEYPIECE

COLIN CAMPBELL
Architect

Measured and Drawn by C. J. Woodbridge.

Plate 178   Chimney-pieces

Carved Wood Chimneypiece, from the Old Rolls Office

Ins 12 6 9   1   2   3   4   5   6   7 Ft

From the OLD ROLLS OFFICE
Chancery Lane

COLIN CAMPBELL
Architect

Measured and Drawn by C. J. Woodbridge.

Plate 180

Chimney-pieces.

Left-Hand Half.

Centre Line.

Right-Hand Half.

Centre Line.

Carved Wood Chimneypiece, from the Old Rolls Office, Chancery Lane, London: Details of Cartouche and Drop in Broken Pediment.

Measured and Drawn by C. J. Woodbridge.

Chimneypiece in Registrar General's Office, Somerset House, London.

Plate 182   Chimney-pieces

SOMERSET HOVSE   CHIMNEYPIECE   SIR WILLIAM CHAMBERS

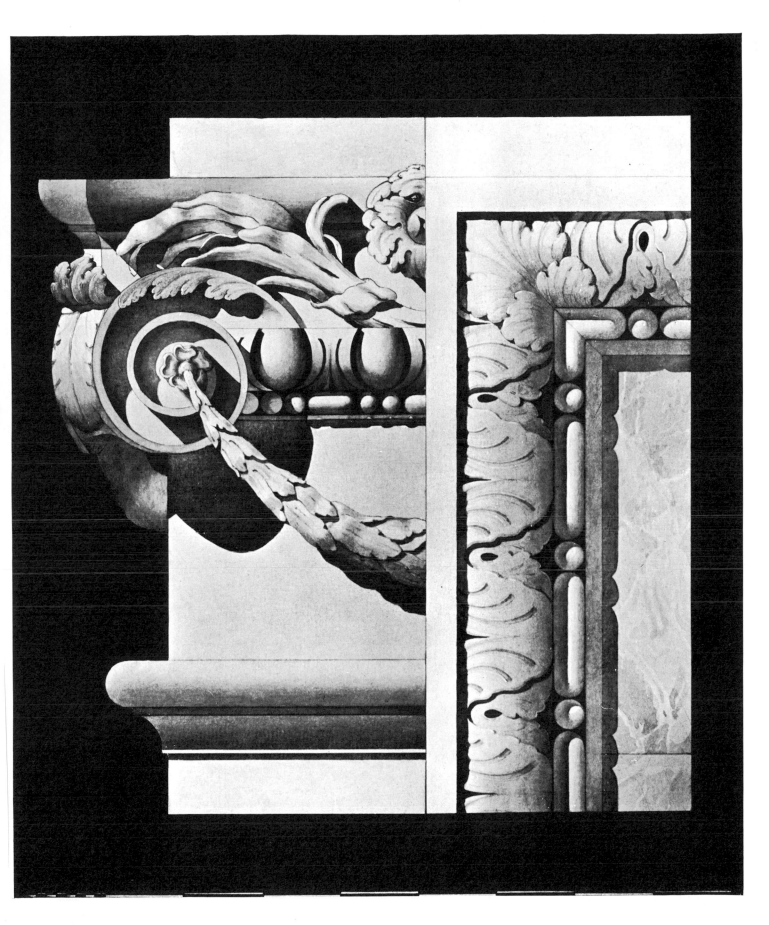

Detail of Chimneypiece in Registrar General's Office, Somerset House, London.

Measured and Drawn by C. J. Woodbridge.

Plate 184   Chimney-pieces

Marble Chimneypiece in the Library, Somerset House, London.

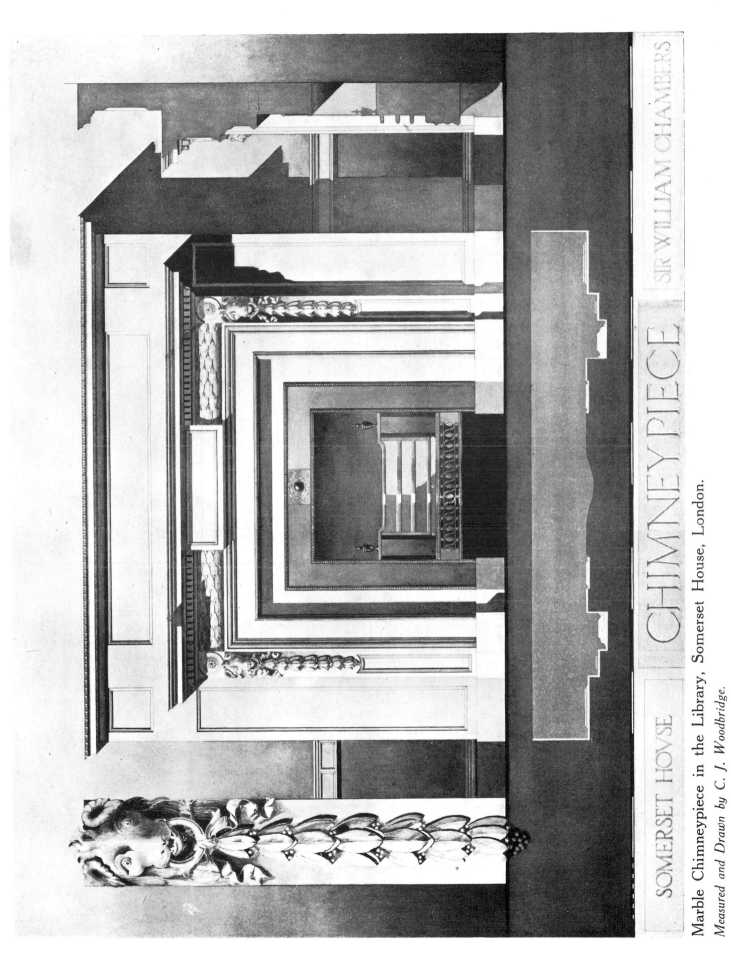

SOMERSET HOVSE   CHIMNEYPIECE   SIR WILLIAM CHAMBERS

Marble Chimneypiece in the Library, Somerset House, London.

Measured and Drawn by C. J. Woodbridge.

Plate 186

Chimney-pieces.

A Chimney-piece at 10, Henrietta Street, Dublin.

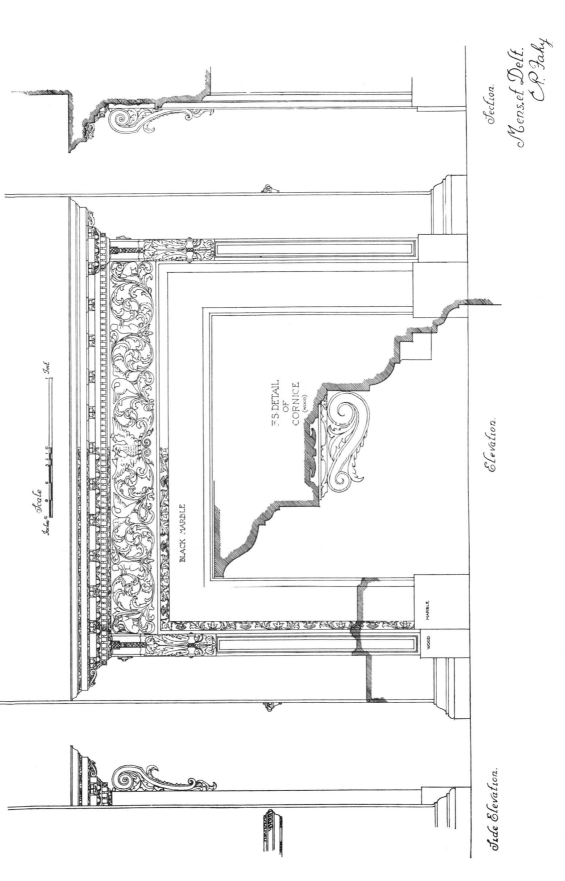

A Chimney-piece at 10, Henrietta Street, Dublin.

Measured and Drawn by C. P. Fahy.

Plate 188   Chimney-pieces

Fireplace, formerly at No. 26, Hatton Garden

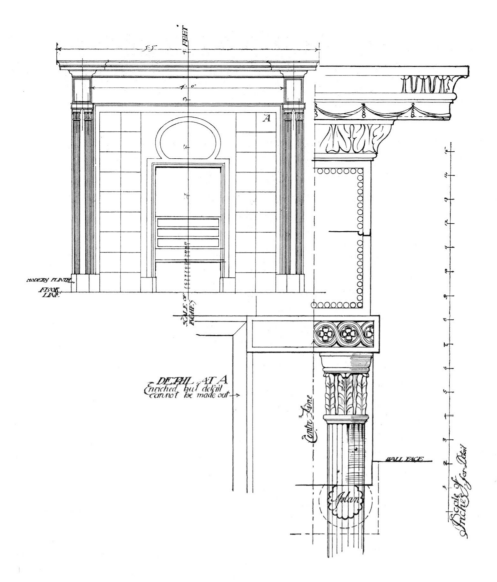

Fireplace, formerly at No. 26, Hatton Garden, City of London.

Measured and Drawn by J. M. W. Halley.

Plate 190   Chimney-pieces

Chimney-piece at the Soane Museum, 13, Lincoln's Inn Fields

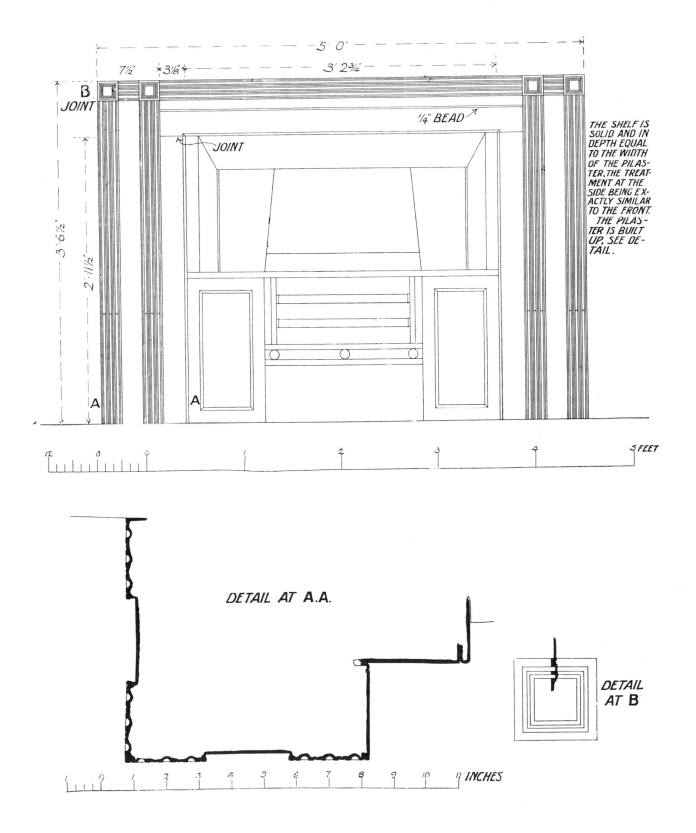

THE SHELF IS SOLID AND IN DEPTH EQUAL TO THE WIDTH OF THE PILASTER, THE TREATMENT AT THE SIDE BEING EXACTLY SIMILAR TO THE FRONT. THE PILASTER IS BUILT UP, SEE DETAIL.

DETAIL AT A.A.

DETAIL AT B

Chimney-piece at the Soane Museum, 13, Lincoln's Inn Fields

Measured and Drawn by Francis Bacon.

Staircases

Notes on Plates 192—212

Plates 192–198

Cromwell House, Highgate, London.

The house was built on Highgate Hill in 1637–40. It is a red brick building with a lot of attractive brick decoration. The staircase is one of the first in London to have had a handrail supported not by balusters but by panels of cut-out decoration. The strapwork is very rich, with emblems of war matching the mood of the figures carved on the newel posts who are supposed to represent types of soldiers in Cromwell's Model Army. The staircase goes right up to the second floor in a lofty narrow well.

Plates 199–200

House formerly in Botolph Lane, London.

A comparison of this seventeenth-century staircase with the ones shown later demonstrates the differences characterizing seventeenth-century and eighteenth-century work. The very vigorous mouldings and decoration, the carving on the balusters and the sturdy design of the doorway on the landing give an effect of marked virility to this staircase. The same applies, also, to the preceding example—that at Cromwell House, of about the same date. In the case of the eighteenth-century staircases which follow later, the detailing is more elegant and far less robust.

This staircase was demolished many years ago.

Plates 201–204

St Anselm's, formerly at Croydon, Surrey.

These plates show views and drawings of the staircase and panelling of the staircase hall of the Queen Anne house illustrated in *Plates 65, 66*. The house was built in 1708 but was destroyed by enemy action in 1940. This was a very finely executed staircase. Note the balusters which are in groups of three, repeated up the staircase. Each one of the three balusters has a different design.

Plates 205–207

Brent House, formerly at Brentford, London.

Oak staircase of the eighteenth century. The house was demolished many years ago. Although standard in plan, the carving on this staircase was exceptionally good. The cut strings and delicate balusters, as well as the carved newels and ramps, make this staircase noteworthy.

Plates 208–210

Hooe Manor, near Plymouth, Devon.

Hooe Manor is situated west of Plymstock, near Plymouth. It was built in the eighteenth century and is notable for the graceful contemporary staircase illustrated here, with its beautifully carved detailing. This staircase has been attributed to Adam.

Plates 211–212

Formerly at 28 Margaret Street, London.

This is a good example of a simple eighteenth-century London staircase. The whole is made of oak. The balusters are arranged in threes and the spandrels are well carved. This staircase was re-erected in the country when the house was demolished.

Staircase, Cromwell House, London.

Plate 193

Staircases.

Staircase, Cromwell House, London.

On the newel posts are the figures of soldiers of Cromwell's Model Army

STAIRCASE
CROMWELL HOUSE
HIGHGATE
·LONDON·N·

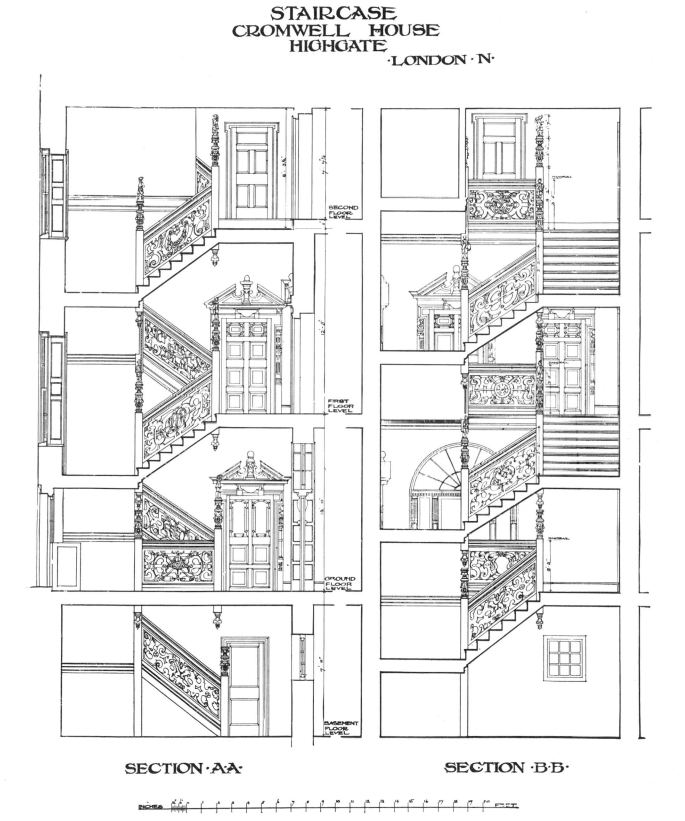

SECTION ·A·A·   SECTION ·B·B·

Measured and Drawn by William Dean, A.R.I.B.A.

Plate 195   Staircases.

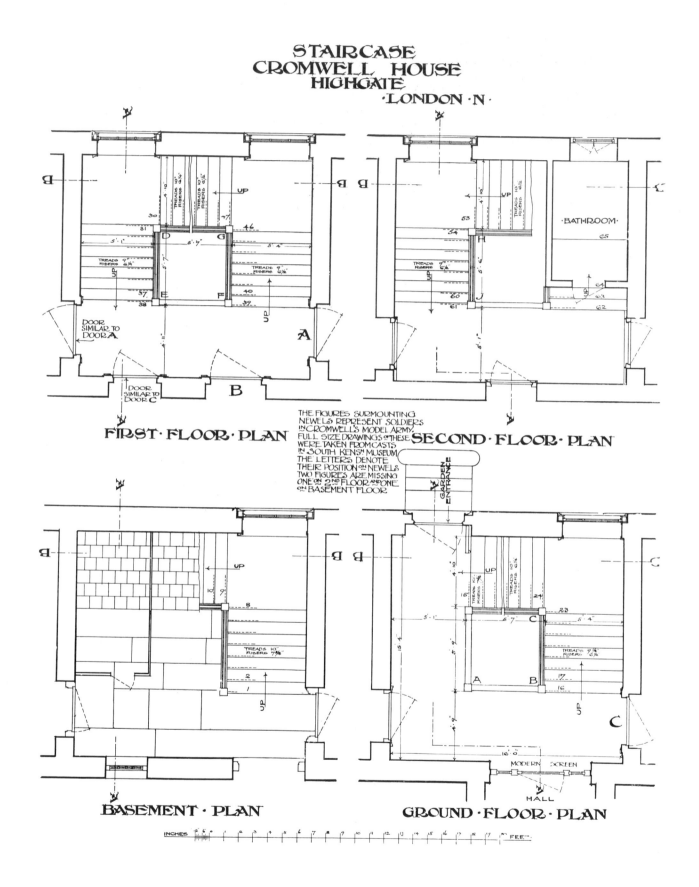

STAIRCASE
CROMWELL HOUSE
HIGHGATE
·LONDON·N·

FIRST·FLOOR·PLAN

SECOND·FLOOR·PLAN

THE FIGURES SURMOUNTING
NEWELS REPRESENT SOLDIERS
IN CROMWELL'S MODEL ARMY.
FULL SIZE DRAWINGS OF THESE
WERE TAKEN FROM CASTS
IN SOUTH KEN^SN MUSEUM.
THE LETTERS DENOTE
THEIR POSITION ON NEWELS.
TWO FIGURES ARE MISSING
ONE ON 2ND FLOOR AND ONE
ON BASEMENT FLOOR.

BASEMENT·PLAN

GROUND·FLOOR·PLAN

Measured and Drawn by William Dean, A.R.I.B.A.

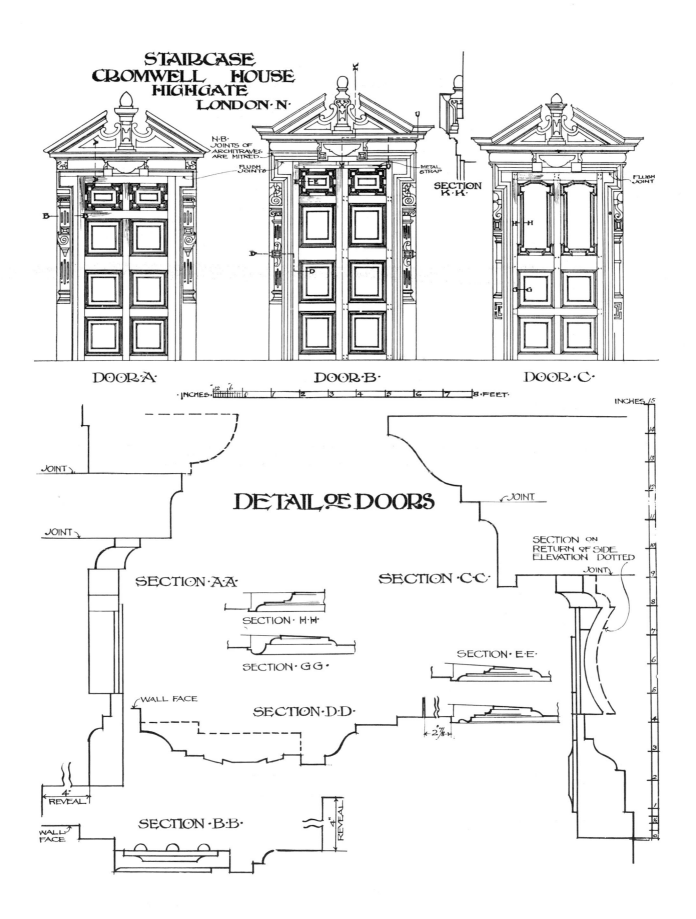

STAIRCASE
CROMWELL HOUSE
HIGHGATE
LONDON·N·

N·B·
JOINTS OF
ARCHITRAVES
ARE MITRED

FLUSH
JOINTS

METAL
STRAP

SECTION·K·K·

FLUSH
JOINT

DOOR·A· DOOR·B· DOOR·C·

·INCHES· 12 6 0 1 2 3 4 5 6 7 8·FEET·

DETAIL OF DOORS

INCHES 15

JOINT

JOINT

JOINT

SECTION·A·A· SECTION·C·C·

SECTION ON
RETURN OF SIDE
ELEVATION DOTTED

JOINT

SECTION·H·H·

SECTION·G·G·

SECTION·E·E·

WALL FACE

SECTION·D·D·

2⅞"

4"
REVEAL

WALL
FACE

SECTION·B·B·

4"
REVEAL

Measured and Drawn by William Dean, A.R.I.B.A.

Plate 197

Staircases.

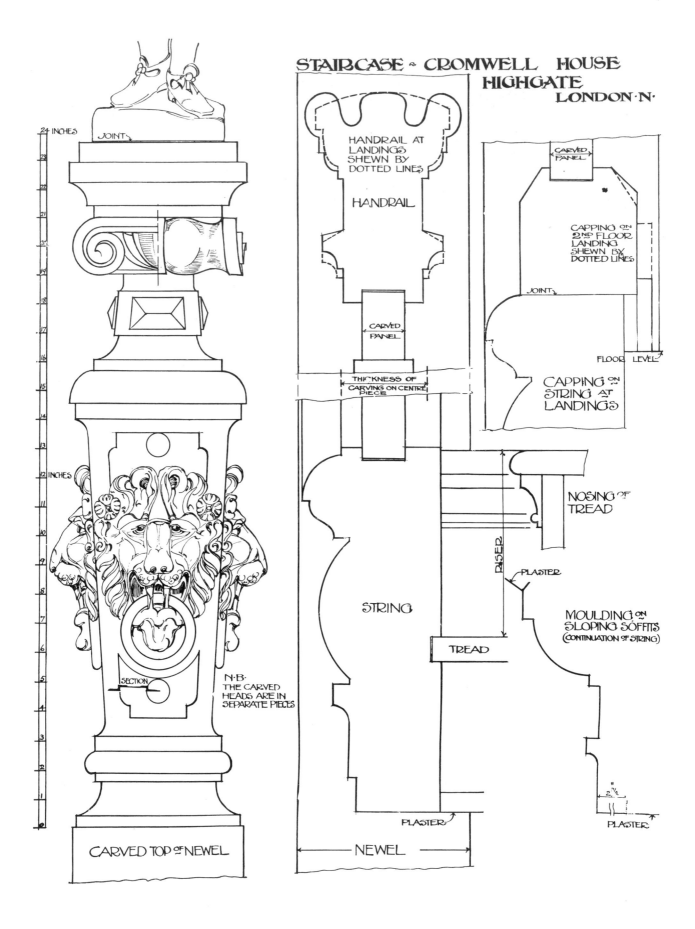

STAIRCASE ~ CROMWELL HOUSE HIGHGATE LONDON·N·

24 INCHES

JOINT

HANDRAIL AT LANDINGS SHEWN BY DOTTED LINES

HANDRAIL

CARVED PANEL

CARVED PANEL

CAPPING ON 2ND FLOOR LANDING SHEWN BY DOTTED LINES

JOINT

FLOOR LEVEL

CAPPING ON STRING AT LANDINGS

THICKNESS OF CARVING ON CENTRE PIECE

12 INCHES

NOSING OF TREAD

RISER

PLASTER

STRING

SECTION

N·B· THE CARVED HEADS ARE IN SEPARATE PIECES

MOULDING ON SLOPING SOFFITS (CONTINUATION OF STRING)

TREAD

2"½

PLASTER

PLASTER

CARVED TOP OF NEWEL

NEWEL

Measured and Drawn by William Dean, A.R.I.B.A.

STAIRCASE
CROMWELL
HOUSE
HIGHGATE
LONDON · N ·

DETAIL OF PANELS

PENDANT ON NEWELS.

DETAIL OF PANELS

Measured and Drawn by William Dean, A.R I.B.A.

House (now demolished) in Botolph Lane, City of London

NOTE.—The three doors on this landing are alike.   This view is of the one on the opposite side of the landing to that shown in the drawings.

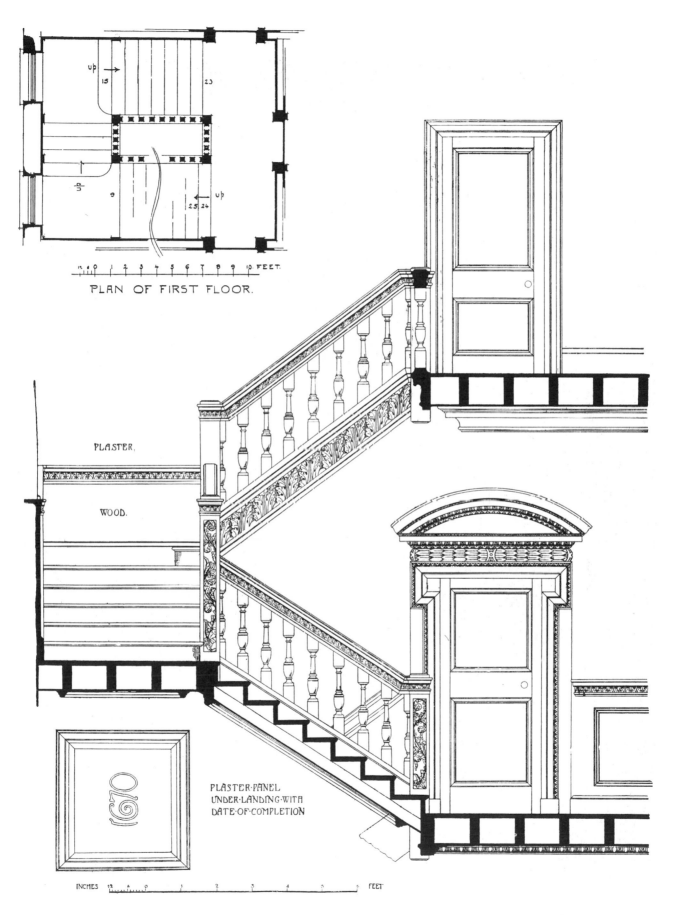

PLAN OF FIRST FLOOR.

PLASTER.

WOOD.

PLASTER·PANEL
UNDER·LANDING·WITH
DATE·OF·COMPLETION

Door, 1st floor landing, of House (now demolished), Botolph Lane, City of London

Measured and Drawn by Norman Jewson.

Plate 201

Staircases.

The Staircase, St. Anselm's Preparatory School, Croydon, Surrey.

The First Floor Landing.

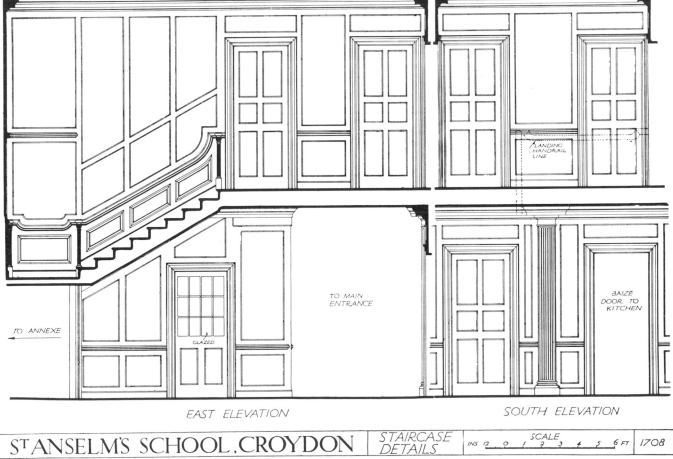

TO ANNEXE

GLAZED

TO MAIN ENTRANCE

LANDING HANDRAIL LINE

BAIZE DOOR TO KITCHEN

EAST ELEVATION

SOUTH ELEVATION

ST ANSELM'S SCHOOL, CROYDON | STAIRCASE DETAILS | SCALE INS 12 0 1 2 3 4 5 6 FT | 1708

The Upper Half of the Staircase.

Measured and Drawn by Christopher J. Woodbridge.

Plate 203

Staircases.

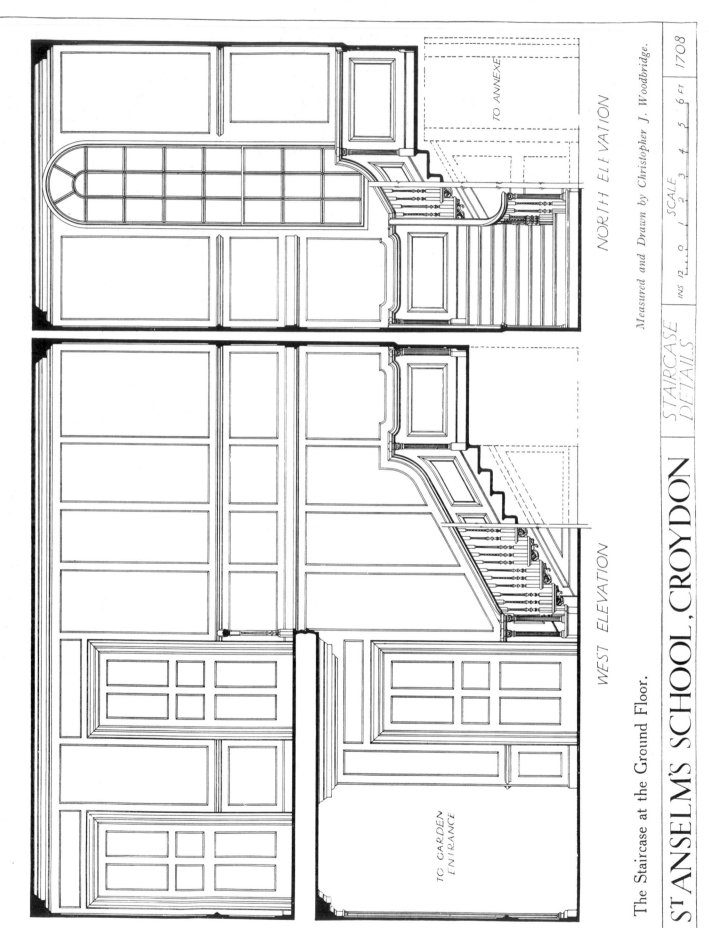

NORTH ELEVATION

WEST ELEVATION

TO ANNEXE

TO GARDEN ENTRANCE

Measured and Drawn by Christopher J. Woodbridge.

SCALE

INS 12 0 1 2 3 4 5 6 FT

1708

STAIRCASE DETAILS

The Staircase at the Ground Floor.

ST ANSELM'S SCHOOL, CROYDON

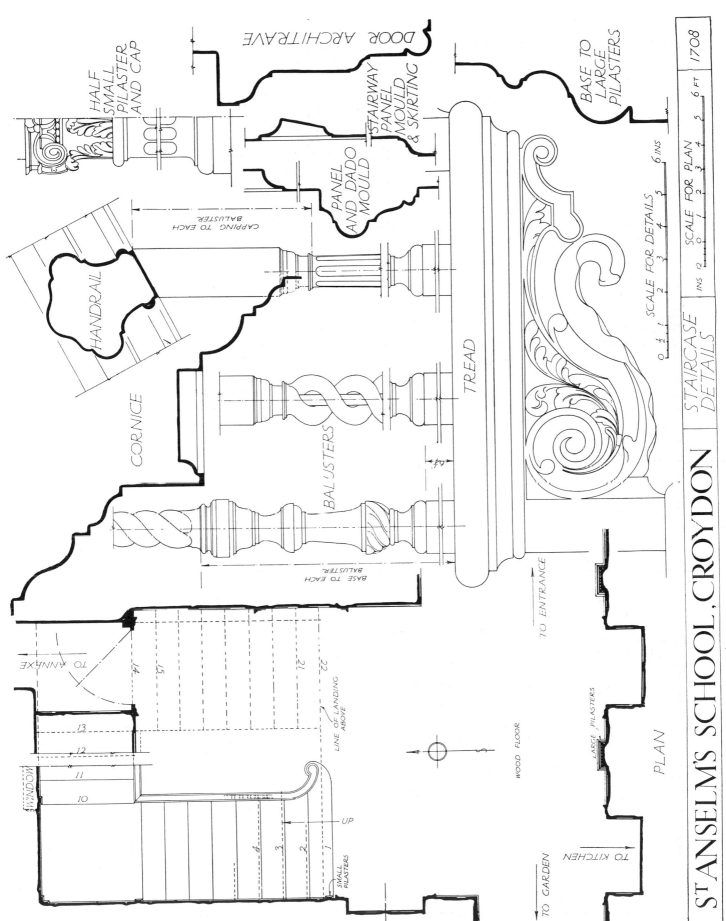

HALF SMALL PILASTER AND CAP

DOOR ARCHITRAVE

STAIRWAY PANEL MOULD & SKIRTING

BASE TO LARGE PILASTERS

PANEL AND DADO MOULD

CAPPING TO EACH BALUSTER

HANDRAIL

CORNICE

BALUSTERS

BASE TO EACH BALUSTER

TREAD

TO ENTRANCE

SCALE FOR DETAILS

6 INS

SCALE FOR PLAN

1708

0   ½   1   2   3   4   5   6 FT

INS   12

LINE OF LANDING ABOVE

TO ANNEXE

13   12   11   10

WINDOW

UP

SMALL PILASTERS

14   15   21   22

WOOD FLOOR

TO GARDEN   TO KITCHEN

LARGE PILASTERS

PLAN

ST ANSELM'S SCHOOL, CROYDON   STAIRCASE DETAILS

Measured and Drawn by Christopher J. Woodbridge.

Plate 205   Staircases.

Eighteenth-Century Oak Staircase, Brent House, Brentford, Middlesex

*A plan of the hall and a section (showing the entrance and the
fenestration on the front elevation) are illustrated in Plate 207.*

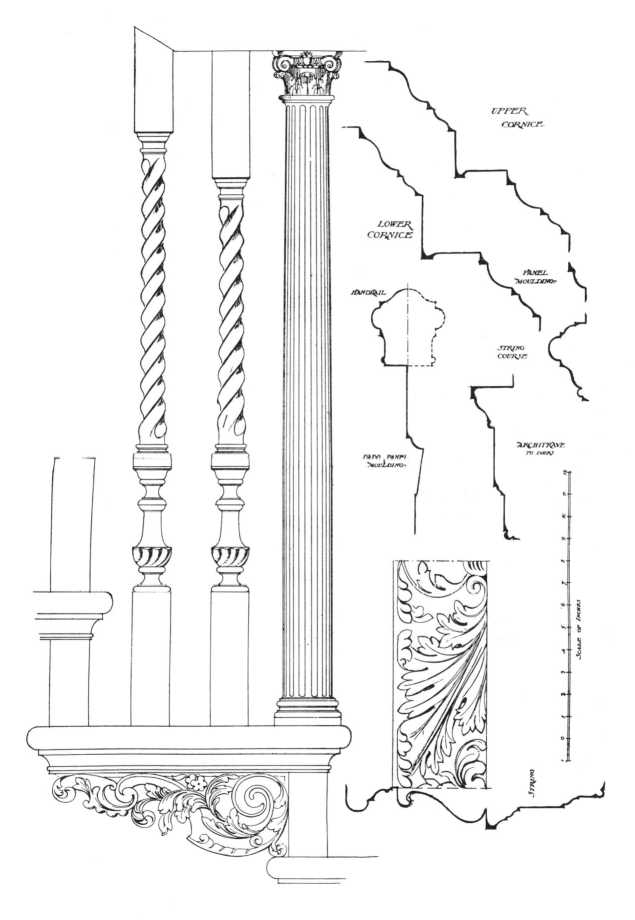

UPPER
CORNICE.

LOWER
CORNICE

PANEL
MOULDING:

HANDRAIL

STRING
COURSE

MAIN PANEL
MOULDING:

ARCHITRAVE
TO DOOR

SCALE OF INCHES

STRING

Detail of Staircase, Brent House, Brentford, Middlesex.

Measured and Drawn by R. L. Wall, A.R.I.B.A.

Plate 207

Staircases.

GROUND FLOOR PLAN.

LANDING.

5' 2½'

ENTRANCE HALL.
BLACK and WHITE MARBLE FLOORING.

18' 4½'

20' 2'

SCALE OF FEET.

0 1 2 3 4 5 6 7 8 9 10 11 12 13 14 15 16 17 18 19 20

SECTION C.C.

STAIRCASE formerly at
BRENT HOUSE.

Measured and Drawn by R. L. Walt, A.R.I.B.A.

Staircase at Hooe Manor, near Plymouth.

Plate 209   Staircases.

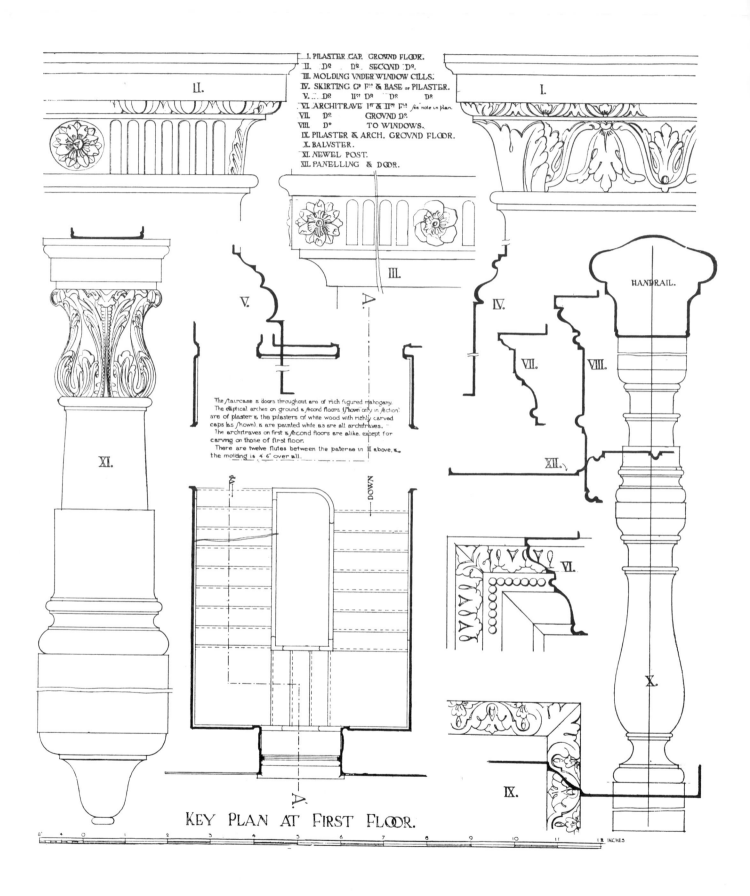

I. PILASTER CAP. GROUND FLOOR.
II. Dº . Dº . SECOND Dº.
III. MOLDING UNDER WINDOW CILLS.
IV. SKIRTING Gᵈ Fʳ & BASE ᵒᶠ PILASTER.
V. Dº . IIᵗ Dº . Dº . Dº
VI. ARCHITRAVE Iᵗ & IIᵗ Fʳ see note in plan.
VII. Dº . GROUND Dº.
VIII. Dº . TO WINDOWS.
IX. PILASTER & ARCH. GROUND FLOOR.
X. BALVSTER.
XI. NEWEL POST.
XII. PANELLING & DOOR.

The staircase & doors throughout are of rich figured mahogany.
The elliptical arches on ground & second floors (shown only in section)
are of plaster & the pilasters of white wood with richly carved
caps (as shown), & are painted white as are all architraves.
The architraves on first & second floors are alike, except for
carving on those of first floor.
There are twelve flutes between the pateras in III above, &
the molding is 4′6″ over all.

HANDRAIL.

KEY PLAN AT FIRST FLOOR.

Staircase at Hooe Manor, near Plymouth.   *Measured and Drawn by William Bruce Bailey.*

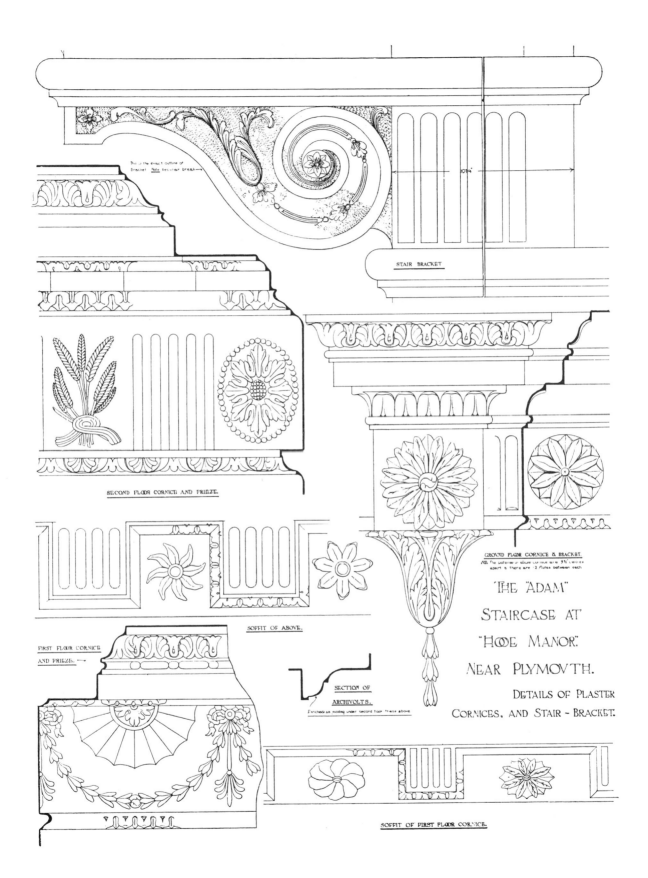

STAIR BRACKET

SECOND FLOOR CORNICE AND FRIEZE.

SOFFIT OF ABOVE.

FIRST FLOOR CORNICE AND FRIEZE.

SECTION OF ARCHIVOLTS.

GROUND FLOOR CORNICE & BRACKET.

THE "ADAM"
STAIRCASE AT
"HOOE MANOR"
NEAR PLYMOUTH.
DETAILS OF PLASTER
CORNICES, AND STAIR-BRACKET.

SOFFIT OF FIRST FLOOR CORNICE.

Measured and Drawn by William Bruce Bailey.

The scale is approximately ⅓rd full size.

Plate 211   Staircases.

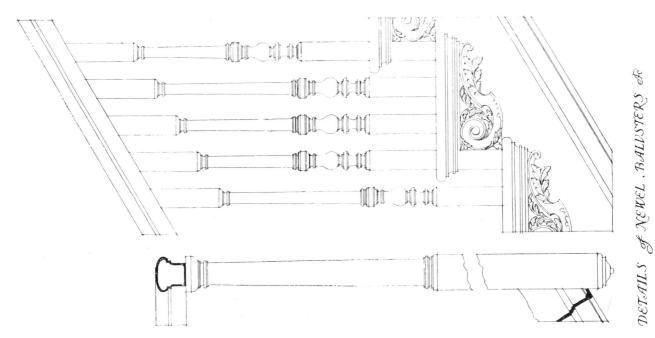

DETAILS of NEWEL, BALUSTERS &c

Oak Staircase formerly at 28 Margaret Street, London, W.

Measured and Drawn by Charles D. Carus Wilson.

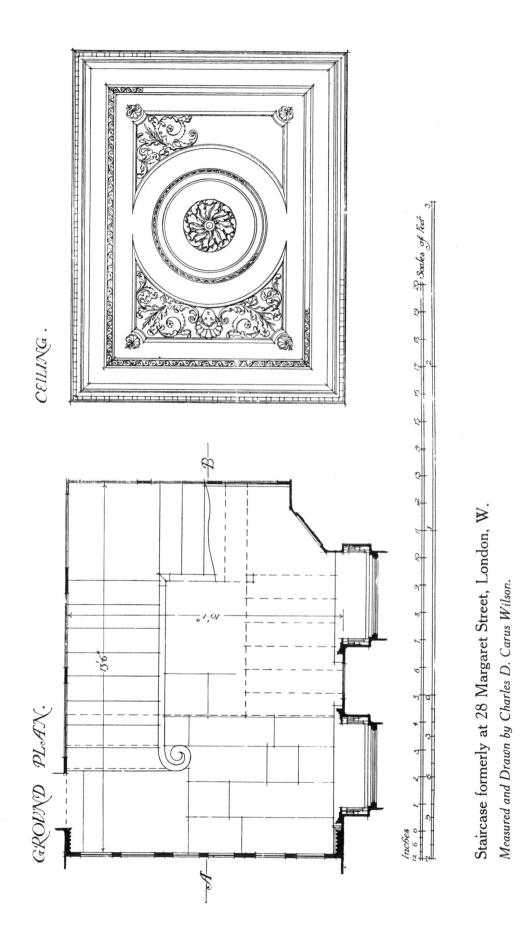

CEILING.

GROUND PLAN.

Staircase formerly at 28 Margaret Street, London, W.

Measured and Drawn by Charles D. Carus Wilson.